KEEP CALM AND BAKE CAKE

A PARTY WITHOUT CAKE IS JUST A MEETING.

JULIA CHILD

KEEP
CALM
AND
BAKE
CAKE

EBURY
PRESS

3 5 7 9 10 8 6 4 2

Published in 2013 by Ebury Press, an imprint of Ebury Publishing

A Random House Group Company

Text and illustrations © Ebury Press 2013

The Random House Group Limited Reg. No. 954009

Addresses for companies within the Random House Group can be found at www.randomhouse.co.uk

A CIP catalogue record for this book is available from the British Library

To buy books by your favourite authors and register for offers visit www.randomhouse.co.uk

Project editor: Roxanne Mackey

Design: Lucy Stephens

Additional recipe writing: Catherine Phipps

Production: Lucy Harrison

Thanks to Eleanor Cornford and Kate Moore for recipes on pages 70–1 and 170–1 respectively

Printed and bound by CPI Group (UK) Ltd, Croydon, CR0 4YY

ISBN 978-0-0919-5566-3

THERE IS NO LOVE SINCERER THAN THE LOVE OF FOOD.

GEORGE BERNARD SHAW

WHERE THERE IS CAKE, THERE IS HOPE. AND THERE IS ALWAYS CAKE.

DEAN
KOONTZ

CONTENTS

COMPOSED CHOCOLATE

Chocolate Brownies with Spiced Oranges

These gooey squares are enriched with melting chunks of chocolate and served with a cool spiced orange compôte.

MAKES 16

125g skinned hazelnuts

125g unsalted butter

175g dark chocolate (at least 70% cocoa solids)

175g light muscovado sugar

2 eggs, beaten

a few drops of vanilla extract

50g plain white flour

a pinch of salt

1 tsp baking powder

1. Preheat the oven to 180°C/Gas 4. Grease and line an 18cm square baking tin (see page 212), making sure that the paper extends 5cm above the rim. Bake the hazelnuts on a baking tray for 15–20 minutes until browned. Cool, then chop coarsely.

2. Melt the butter with 50g of the chocolate, broken into pieces, in a heatproof bowl over a pan of simmering water (see page 218). Place the sugar, eggs and vanilla extract in a large bowl, then sift in the flour, salt

FOR THE SPICED ORANGES

125g caster sugar

½ cinnamon stick

2 cloves

1 star anise

3 oranges

TO FINISH

1 tbsp icing sugar,
   for dusting

and baking powder. Pour in the melted mixture and stir gently, until well mixed.

3. Roughly chunk the remaining chocolate and stir into the brownie mixture, with the hazelnuts. Spoon into the prepared tin and spread evenly. Bake in the oven for 50 minutes or until the cake begins to shrink from the sides of the tin and the centre is springy to the touch.

4. Meanwhile, for the oranges, place the sugar in a pan with 150ml water and dissolve over a low heat, stirring occasionally. Add the spices and bring to the boil. Boil for 2 minutes, then remove from the heat.

5. Working on a plate to catch the juices, remove the peel and all the white pith from the oranges. Cut into 0.5cm thick slices and place in a bowl. Pour on the syrup, with any orange juice. Leave to cool.

6. Leave the cake to cool in the tin for 30 minutes. Turn out and cut into 16 squares and dust with a little icing sugar. Serve the brownies warm, with the spiced oranges.

COMPOSED CHOCOLATE

THERE ARE
FOUR BASIC
FOOD GROUPS:
MILK CHOCOLATE,
DARK CHOCOLATE,
WHITE CHOCOLATE
AND CHOCOLATE
TRUFFLES.

ANON

WHITE CHOCOLATE BROWNIES

DELICIOUSLY MOIST, LADEN WITH WHITE CHOCOLATE AND CRUSTED IN A GLOSSY COAT OF SUGAR, THESE WHITE CHOCOLATE BROWNIES MAKE AN ADORABLE TEATIME TREAT!

MAKES 20

500g white chocolate

75g unsalted butter

3 eggs

175g caster sugar

175g self-raising white flour

a pinch of salt

175g skinned hazelnuts, roughly chopped

1 tsp vanilla extract

1. Preheat the oven to 190°C/Gas 5. Grease and line a baking tin measuring 21cm x 28cm (see page 212).

2. Roughly chop 400g of the chocolate and set aside. Break up the remaining chocolate and put it in a heatproof bowl with the butter. Place over a pan of simmering water until melted (see page 218). Leave to cool slightly.

3. Whisk the eggs and sugar together in a large bowl until smooth, then

VARIATIONS

YOU CAN USE OTHER ROUGHLY CHOPPED NUTS INSTEAD OF THE HAZELNUTS. ALMONDS, WALNUTS, PECANS AND BRAZIL NUTS ARE SUITABLE.

gradually beat in the melted chocolate mixture. Sift the flour and salt over the mixture, then fold in with the hazelnuts, chopped chocolate and vanilla extract.

4. Turn the mixture into the prepared tin and level the surface. Bake for 30–35 minutes until risen and golden, and the centre is just firm to the touch. Leave to cool in the tin for 30 minutes. Turn out and cut into 20 squares.

Chocolate Blinis with Hazelnut Caramel

OLD-FASHIONED DROP SCONES TAKE ON A NEW LEASE OF LIFE IN THIS PUDDING. THE COMBINATION OF MELTING CHOCOLATE, TANGY NUT CARAMEL AND CREAMY YOGHURT IS SHEER BLISS!

SERVES 6

100g self-raising white flour
15g cocoa powder
½ tsp baking powder
1 tbsp caster sugar
1 egg
200ml milk
75g milk chocolate, roughly chopped
a little oil, for cooking

1. Sift the flour, cocoa powder and baking powder into a bowl. Stir in the sugar. Make a well in the centre and stir in the egg and a little of the milk to make a thick batter. Stir in the remaining milk and the chopped chocolate. Leave to stand while making the sauce.

2. Preheat the grill to medium heat. Chop the nuts very roughly and toast on a baking tray, turning frequently,

FOR THE CARAMEL

50g skinned hazelnuts

75g caster sugar

zest of ½ orange

40g unsalted butter

TO SERVE

Greek-style yoghurt

until evenly golden. Put the sugar in a small pan with 90ml water and heat gently until the sugar dissolves, stirring occasionally. Bring to the boil and boil rapidly until deep golden. Immerse the base of the pan in cold water to prevent further cooking.

3. Carefully add 2 tablespoons of water, standing back as the syrup will splutter. Add the hazelnuts, orange zest and butter, and reheat gently until smooth and glossy.

4. Cook the blinis in batches. Heat a little oil in a large, heavy-based frying pan or griddle over a moderate heat. Add dessertspoonfuls of the batter, spacing them well apart. Fry gently for 2 minutes or until bubbles appear on the surface. Flip the blinis over with a palette knife and cook until just firm. Transfer to a warmed plate.

5. Gently reheat the sauce. Transfer the blinis to serving plates, allowing three per serving, and pour a little of the sauce over them. Serve immediately, with yoghurt.

VARIATIONS

USE TOASTED WALNUTS OR ALMONDS IN PLACE OF THE HAZELNUTS AND LEMON INSTEAD OF THE ORANGE ZEST.

BOURBON SALTED CARAMEL BROWNIES

THESE DENSE, CHEWY BROWNIES ARE STRICTLY ADULTS ONLY, THANKS TO THE BOURBON, WHICH NOT ONLY LIFTS THE RICHNESS OF CHOCOLATE, BUT ALSO REALLY ENLIVENS THE SALTED CARAMEL.

MAKES 15–18

175g unsalted butter

250g dark chocolate (at least 70% cocoa solids)

300g light soft brown sugar

4 large eggs

1 tsp vanilla extract

2 tbsp Bourbon

225g plain white flour

1. First make the caramel. Put the sugar in a saucepan and warm over a medium heat. Watch it carefully. When it starts to liquify and turn brown around the edges, gently swirl the pan until the sugar has completely melted and is smoking a little.

2. Remove from the heat and pour in half the cream – it will rise up, so be careful. Stir briskly until it subsides, then add the rest of the cream, the Bourbon, butter and salt. Whisk to

FOR THE CARAMEL

150g caster sugar
100ml double cream
25ml Bourbon
10g unsalted butter
a pinch of sea salt

combine – you may need to return it to the heat to help it even out. Pour into a bowl, cool, then chill in the fridge for 45 minutes.

3. Preheat the oven to 180°C/Gas 4. Grease and line a 30cm x 20cm baking tin (see page 212). Melt the butter in a saucepan, break the chocolate into pieces and add it to the butter. Stir over a very low heat until completely melted. Remove from the heat and stir in the sugar and then the eggs, one at a time. Add the vanilla extract, the Bourbon and then the flour.

4. Beat the mixture until thoroughly combined and the batter is thick and glossy. Pour half the batter into the prepared tin. Dot with spoonfuls of the caramel, then smooth over the remaining brownie batter. Use a palette knife to swirl the caramel lightly – do not over-swirl, otherwise the brownies will not set properly.

5. Bake for 35–40 minutes until the cake is just set. Score the brownies into portions. Leave to cool in the tin for 30 minutes, then turn out and cut when completely cooled.

THE BELLY RULES THE MIND.

SPANISH
PROVERB

I DON'T BELIEVE IN LOW-FAT COOKING.

NIGELLA LAWSON

White Chocolate Fudge Cake

LIGHT SPONGE ROUNDS ARE SANDWICHED TOGETHER WITH WHIPPED CREAM, FLAVOURED WITH WHITE CHOCOLATE AND LEMON JUICE. THE ENTIRE CAKE IS THEN SMOTHERED IN IRRESISTIBLE WHITE CHOCOLATE FUDGE ICING!

SERVES 12

4 eggs

125g caster sugar

finely grated zest of 1 lemon

125g plain white flour

50g white chocolate, finely grated

FOR THE FILLING

50g white chocolate

150ml double cream

5 tsp lemon juice

1. Preheat the oven to 180°C/Gas 4. Grease and line a 19cm round cake tin (see page 212).

2. Put the eggs, sugar and lemon zest in a large heatproof bowl over a pan of hot water and whisk until the mixture has doubled in volume and is thick enough to leave a trail on the surface when the whisk is lifted. Remove the bowl from the pan and leave to cool.

FOR THE ICING

175g white chocolate
125g unsalted butter
4 tbsp milk
175g icing sugar

TO FINISH

1 tbsp cocoa powder
   or icing sugar,
   for dusting

3. Sift the flour over the mixture, then sprinkle with the grated chocolate. Fold in lightly, using a large metal spoon. Scrape into the prepared tin and bake for 30–35 minutes, until just firm to the touch. Turn out and cool on a wire rack.

4. For the filling, chop the chocolate into small pieces. Whip the cream until it just holds its shape. Stir in the chocolate and lemon juice.

5. Split the sponge horizontally into two layers and sandwich together with the filling. Place on a serving plate.

6. For the icing, break up the chocolate and put into a pan with the butter and milk. Heat gently until dissolved, then stir until smooth. Beat in the icing sugar.

7. Allow the icing to cool, then beat until it forms soft peaks. Spread over the top and sides of the cake. Dust with cocoa powder or icing sugar just before serving.

CHOCOLATE ROULADE WITH FRUIT COMPÔTE

THIS CLASSIC DARK ROULADE IS FILLED WITH LIGHTLY SWEETENED CREAM AND FROMAGE FRAIS, SCATTERED WITH SOFT FRUITS AND SERVED IN THICK SLICES WITH SUMMER FRUIT COMPÔTE.

SERVES 8–10

125g dark chocolate (at least 70% cocoa solids)

4 eggs, separated

125g caster sugar, plus extra for sprinkling

2 tbsp cocoa powder, sifted

FOR THE FILLING

200ml double cream

90ml plain fromage frais

2 tbsp icing sugar

1. Preheat the oven to 180°C/Gas 4. Grease and line a 23cm x 33cm Swiss roll tin with non-stick baking parchment (see page 213).

2. To make the roulade, break the chocolate into pieces and melt it in a heatproof bowl over a pan of hot water (see page 218). Stir, then leave to cool slightly. Whisk the egg yolks and sugar in a large bowl over a pan of hot water until very thick and creamy. Beat in the chocolate.

FOR THE COMPÔTE

250g blackberries

50g caster sugar

150g redcurrants

225g raspberries

2 tbsp crème de cassis liqueur (optional)

3. Whisk the egg whites in a bowl to stiff peaks, then fold into the chocolate mixture with the cocoa powder. Pour into the prepared tin and spread evenly. Bake for about 20 minutes until risen and firm to the touch.

4. Meanwhile, generously sprinkle a sheet of non-stick baking parchment with caster sugar. Turn out the roulade onto the paper and peel off the lining paper. Cover with a damp tea towel and leave to cool.

5. To make the compôte, put the blackberries and sugar in a small pan and cook over a low heat for 5-8 minutes until just soft. Remove from heat, add the redcurrants and allow to cool.

6. Transfer one-third of the fruit to a bowl, using a slotted spoon. Add 50g of the raspberries and set aside for the filling. Press the remaining raspberries through a sieve and stir into the fruit compôte in the pan, with the liqueur (if using).

7. When the roulade is cold, whip the cream to soft peaks and fold in the

NOTE

DON'T WORRY IF THE ROULADE CRACKS SLIGHTLY AS YOU ROLL IT, THE CRACKS ARE PART OF ITS CHARM!

fromage frais and icing sugar. Carefully spread over the roulade, then scatter over the fruit filling. Roll up from one of the narrow ends, using the paper to help. Transfer the roulade to a board and dust generously with icing sugar.

Spoon the red fruit compôte onto individual plates and top with a slice of the roulade.

COMPOSED CHOCOLATE

COOKING IS LIKE LOVE, IT SHOULD BE ENTERED INTO WITH ABANDON OR NOT AT ALL.

HARRIET VAN HORNE

Double Chocolate Muffins

These decadent muffins are richly flavoured with melted chocolate. Additional chunks of dark and white chocolate are folded in before baking too. These give melt-in-the-mouth bites of pure delight!

MAKES 12

- 300g dark chocolate (at least 70% cocoa solids)
- 125g white chocolate
- 375g self-raising white flour
- 1 tbsp baking powder
- 65g cocoa powder
- 75g light muscovado sugar
- 1 egg

1. Preheat the oven to 220°C/Gas 7. Line a 12-cup muffin tin with paper cases. Break up 175g of the dark chocolate and melt in a heatproof bowl set over a pan of simmering water (see page 218).

2. Roughly chop the remaining dark and white chocolate. Sift the flour, baking powder and cocoa powder into a bowl. Stir in the sugar.

1 egg yolk
2 tsp vanilla extract
6 tbsp vegetable oil
375ml milk

TO FINISH
1 tbsp icing sugar or
    cocoa powder, for
    dusting (optional)

3. In another bowl, beat together the egg, egg yolk, vanilla extract, oil and milk. Add to the dry ingredients with the chopped chocolate and stir the ingredients together quickly until the flour is only just incorporated; do not over-mix.

4. Spoon the mixture into the paper cases, piling it up in the centre. Bake for 25 minutes until the muffins are well risen and craggy in appearance. Transfer to a wire rack and dust lightly with icing sugar or cocoa powder, if desired. Serve warm or cold.

NOTE

UNLIKE SMALL SPONGE CAKES, THE MUFFIN MIXTURE SHOULD VIRTUALLY FILL THE CASES BEFORE COOKING TO ACHIEVE THE TRADITIONAL 'TOP-HAT' SHAPE.

Dark Chocolate Cake With Brandied Fruit

Under the disguise of a smooth, cream coating is a wickedly rich cake. Moist plump prunes, steeped in a brandy-flavoured syrup, are layered between the dark chocolate sponge rounds.

SERVES 8–10

75g dark chocolate (at least 70% cocoa solids)

175g unsalted butter, softened

300g light muscovado sugar

3 eggs

300g plain white flour

1 tsp bicarbonate of soda

2 tsp baking powder

150ml sour cream

1. Preheat the oven to 190°C/Gas 5. Grease and base line three 20cm round sandwich tins (see page 212). Break up the chocolate and heat very gently in a saucepan with 150ml water until melted. Cool slightly.

2. Cream together the butter and sugar in a bowl until light and fluffy. Gradually beat in the eggs, a little at a time, adding a little of the flour to prevent curdling.

FOR THE FILLING

175g no-need-to-soak
  dried prunes
1 tsp vanilla extract
½ tsp cornflour
90ml brandy

TO DECORATE

450ml double cream
250ml crème fraîche
cocoa powder,
  for dusting

3. Sift together the remaining flour, bicarbonate of soda and baking powder.

4. Stir the chocolate into the creamed mixture, then fold in the flour and sour cream. Divide between the prepared tins and level the surfaces. Bake for 25–30 minutes until firm to touch. Turn out and cool on a wire rack.

5. For the filling, roughly chop the prunes and place in a saucepan with 90ml water and the vanilla extract. Bring to the boil, reduce the heat and simmer gently for 5 minutes. Blend the cornflour with 1 tablespoon of water, add to the pan and cook, stirring, for 1 minute until thickened. Remove from the heat and add the brandy. Leave to cool. For the decoration, whip the cream until just holding its shape. Fold in the crème fraîche.

6. Spread the prune filling on two of the sponges, then cover with a little of the cream. Assemble the three layers on a serving plate and cover with the remaining cream, swirling it attractively. Dust with cocoa powder just before serving.

NOTE

THE PRUNE FILLING, ONCE COOLED, SHOULD BE VERY MOIST, WITH JUICES STILL VISIBLE. ADD A LITTLE EXTRA BRANDY OR WATER IF IT HAS BECOME DRY.

Devil's Food Cake

AS THE NAME IMPLIES, THIS IS A DANGEROUSLY
MOREISH CAKE. IT'S MOIST, LADEN WITH
CHOCOLATE AND LIGHTENED BY THE
BUTTERMILK, WHICH MEANS A SECOND SLICE
IS REALLY HARD TO RESIST ...

SERVES 8–10

300g self-raising
  white flour
75g cocoa powder
2 tsp vanilla extract
100ml buttermilk
250g unsalted
  butter, softened
300g dark
  muscovado sugar
4 large eggs

1. Preheat the oven to 180°C/Gas 4.
Grease and base line three 20cm round
sandwich tins (see page 212). Sift the
flour into a bowl.

2. Dissolve the cocoa powder in
120ml freshly boiled water. Whisk in
the vanilla extract and the buttermilk.

3. Beat the butter and sugar together
in a large bowl with an electric whisk
until very soft and fluffy. Mix in the
eggs one at a time, alternating with

FOR THE FROSTING

150g dark chocolate (at least 70% cocoa solids)

150g unsalted butter

400g icing sugar

1 tsp vanilla extract

75ml milk

tablespoons of the flour. Gently fold in the rest of the flour followed by the chocolate mixture.

4. Divide the batter between the prepared tins. Bake for 20–25 minutes, until the cakes are well risen and firm to the touch. Leave to cool in their tins for 10 minutes, then turn out on to a wire rack.

5. To make the frosting, break the chocolate into pieces and melt it in a heatproof bowl over a pan of simmering water (see page 218). Beat together the butter and icing sugar, then trickle in the melted chocolate and the vanilla. Trickle in the milk, then beat for several minutes until very light, fluffy and doubled in volume.

6. To assemble the cake, sandwich the three layers together with a thick spread of the frosting then use the rest to coat the surface and sides entirely.

Iced Ginger and White Chocolate Cake

Gingerbread crumbs form the basis of a light parfait, which is layered and topped with a tumble of white chocolate ganache, then dusted liberally with a mixture of cocoa powder and icing sugar.

SERVES 8

125g ready-made gingerbread

450ml double cream

125g caster sugar

4 egg yolks

finely grated zest and juice of 1 orange

FOR THE CHOCOLATE GANACHE

300g white chocolate

300ml double cream

1. Line a 20cm spring-release round cake tin (see page 212).

2. To make the chocolate ganache, break the chocolate into a large bowl. Bring the cream to the boil in a small pan, then pour over the chocolate and leave to stand for 5 minutes. Using a large balloon whisk, beat the mixture until smooth. Chill in the fridge until thick.

TO FINISH
1 tbsp icing sugar
1 tbsp cocoa powder

3. To make the parfait, crumble the gingerbread into a bowl using your fingers. Add 150ml of the cream and beat well. Chill in the fridge.

4. Put the sugar and 125ml of water in a saucepan over a low heat, stirring occasionally, until the sugar has dissolved. Increase the heat and boil for 2–3 minutes. Place the egg yolks in a large bowl and whisk in the syrup in a steady stream. Continue whisking until the mixture is cold and very thick.

5. Whip the remaining cream in a bowl, and fold into the ginger mixture with the orange zest and juice. Fold in the egg yolk mixture. Freeze the parfait mixture for 30 minutes until semi-firm. Spoon half into the prepared tin and smooth the surface.

6. Beat the chocolate ganache lightly until smooth, then put into a piping bag fitted with a 0.5cm plain nozzle. Pipe half of the ganache in a tumbling pattern over the ginger parfait. Spoon over the remaining ginger parfait, spread evenly, then pipe over the remaining chocolate ganache.

7. Cover the tin with foil and freeze for 3–4 hours until firm.

8. About 20 minutes before serving, unclip the tin, peel off the paper and transfer the cake to a serving plate. Keep in the fridge until required. Dust with icing sugar and cocoa powder just before serving.

COMPOSED CHOCOLATE

SEIZE THE MOMENT. REMEMBER ALL THOSE WOMEN ON THE TITANIC WHO WAVED OFF THE DESSERT CART.

ERMA BOMBECK

CHOCOLATE FILIGREE CAKES

A DRAMATIC LAYERED CAKE FOR SPECIAL OCCASIONS.

MAKES 16

2 eggs

50g caster sugar

25g self-raising flour

25g cocoa powder

FOR THE FILLING

1 tsp powdered gelatine

100ml milk

200g white chocolate

1 egg

25g caster sugar

1 tsp vanilla extract

250g mascarpone cheese

200g Greek-style yoghurt

TO DECORATE

25g dark chocolate (at least 70% cocoa solids)

1. Preheat the oven to 190°C/Gas 5. Grease and line an 18cm square loose-bottomed cake tin (see page 212).

2. Put the eggs and sugar in a large heatproof bowl over a pan of hot water. Whisk until the mixture has doubled in volume and leaves a trail on the surface when the whisk is lifted. Remove the bowl from the pan and whisk until cool.

3. Sift the flour and cocoa powder, then fold into the mixture. Scrape into the prepared tin and bake for 12–15 minutes until firm to the touch. Turn out and cool on a wire rack.

4. Line the sides of the tin with fresh greaseproof paper (see page 212). Slice the sponge in half horizontally and place one layer in the tin.

5. For the filling, sprinkle the gelatine over the milk in a heatproof bowl and leave for 2–3 minutes. Break up the white chocolate and melt in a heatproof bowl set over a pan of simmering water (see page 218).

6. Whisk the egg, sugar and vanilla extract in a bowl until foamy. Place the bowl containing the gelatine over a pan of simmering water until the gelatine dissolves. Cool slightly, then stir into the white chocolate. Whisk into the egg mixture. Beat in the mascarpone until smooth then fold in the yoghurt.

7. Spoon half the mixture over the sponge in the tin, then cover with the second sponge layer. Top with the remaining mixture. Tap the tin gently to level the surface.

8. Break up the dark chocolate and melt it in a heatproof bowl over a pan of hot water (see page 218). Put it into a piping bag and drizzle fine lines all over the cake surface. Chill until required. Remove from the tin and peel off the paper. Using a hot knife cut the cake into 16 squares.

NOTE

CHILL FOR SEVERAL HOURS OR OVERNIGHT BEFORE SERVING, TO MAKE SLICING EASIER.

CHOCOLATE PECAN FUDGE CAKE

LAYERS OF DARK, MOIST CHOCOLATE CAKE ARE
SANDWICHED TOGETHER WITH WHIPPED CREAM,
TOASTED PECANS AND SWEET MAPLE SYRUP,
THEN SWIRLED WITH CHOCOLATE FUDGE ICING.

SERVES 8–10

175g self-raising
white flour

50g cocoa powder

2 tsp baking powder

175g unsalted butter,
softened

175g caster sugar

4 eggs

2 tsp vanilla extract

1. Preheat the oven to 180°C/Gas 4.
Grease and base line three 20cm round
sandwich tins (see page 212).

2. Sift together the flour, cocoa
powder and baking powder into a bowl.
Add the butter, sugar, eggs and vanilla
extract. Beat, using an electric whisk,
for 2 minutes until smooth. Divide the
mixture between the prepared tins and
level the surfaces. Bake for 25 minutes
until risen and just firm to the touch.
Turn out onto a wire rack to cool.

FOR THE FILLING

300ml double cream

125g pecans,
  roughly chopped

6 tbsp maple syrup

FOR THE ICING

300g dark chocolate
  (at least 70% cocoa
  solids)

50g unsalted butter

4 tbsp milk

225g icing sugar

3. For the filling, whip the cream until just peaking. Place one cake on a serving plate and spread with a quarter of the cream. Scatter over half of the chopped nuts, then drizzle with half of the maple syrup. Spread carefully with another quarter of the cream and position the second cake on top. Cover with the remaining cream, nuts and syrup in the same order, then top with the remaining cake.

4. To make the icing, break up the chocolate and place in a saucepan with the butter and milk. Heat gently until the chocolate is melted, stirring frequently. Remove from the heat and beat in the icing sugar until evenly combined. Leave to cool, then swirl over the top and sides of the cake with a palette knife.

Chocolate Marquise

OUTRAGEOUSLY CHOCOLATEY, THIS SOFT, SMOOTH-TEXTURED MOUSSE IS POURED OVER A CRISP BISCUIT BASE, THEN CHILLED UNTIL SET.

SERVES 8

175g dark chocolate (at least 70% cocoa solids)

3 tbsp strong black coffee

50g unsalted butter

1 tbsp whisky

3 eggs, separated

125g caster sugar

FOR THE BISCUIT BASE

175g chocolate wholemeal biscuits

50g unsalted butter

1. Grease and line a 23cm spring-release round cake tin (see page 212).

2. To make the base, crush the biscuits coarsely in a polythene bag using a rolling pin, or whizz briefly in a food processor. Melt the butter in a saucepan and stir into the biscuit crumbs, until evenly blended in a bowl. Spoon the mixture into the prepared tin and press into an even layer. Set aside.

3. To make the mousse topping, break up the chocolate and place in a heatproof bowl with the coffee, butter

TO DECORATE

75g white chocolate
   curls (optional)
   (see page 219)

3 tbsp cocoa powder,
   for dusting

and whisky. Place the bowl over a pan
of simmering water and leave to melt.
Place the egg yolks and sugar in a large
heatproof bowl over another pan of
simmering water and whisk, using an
electric beater or balloon whisk, until
the mixture is thick and foamy and
leaves a trail on the surface when the
whisk is lifted.

4. Whisk the egg whites in a clean
bowl to soft peaks. Fold the chocolate
mixture into the whisked egg yolk
mixture, then lightly stir in one-third
of the egg whites. Fold in the rest and
pour into the prepared tin. Spread
evenly, then cover and chill in the
fridge overnight.

5. To serve, unclip the tin and peel
away the paper. Carefully transfer
the marquise to a serving plate and
decorate with white chocolate curls,
if desired. Dust liberally with cocoa
powder just before serving.

NOTE

WHEN YOU ARE
MAKING THE CRUMBS
FOR THE BASE, DON'T
PROCESS THEM TOO
FINELY, OTHERWISE
THE BASE WILL BE
DENSE AND HARD.

DREAMY DELIGHTS

CINNAMON CRANBERRY STREUSEL

THIS STREUSEL MOST CLOSELY RESEMBLES SHORTBREAD IN TEXTURE AND IS DELIGHTFUL SERVED, CUT INTO WEDGES, WITH COFFEE.

SERVES 12

350g unsalted butter
75g caster sugar
3 tbsp olive oil
1 tsp vanilla extract
1 large egg
700g plain white flour
1½ tsp baking powder
½ tsp salt
1 tbsp ground cinnamon

FOR THE CRANBERRY SAUCE

225g fresh or frozen cranberries

1. First make the cranberry sauce filling. Place the cranberries in a food processor with the sugar and chop roughly. Transfer to a saucepan and add the orange juice and spice. Bring to the boil, stirring constantly. Lower the heat and simmer for 5 minutes, then set aside to cool completely.

2. To make the streusel dough, cream the butter and sugar together in a bowl until light and fluffy. Beat in the olive oil and vanilla extract. Lightly whisk the egg and beat into the mixture.

75g caster sugar
juice of I orange
½ tsp ground
  mixed spice

TO DECORATE
icing sugar

3. Sift the flour, baking powder, salt and cinnamon into a bowl. Gradually stir into the creamed mixture until the dough resembles a rough shortbread mixture. Bring the dough together with your hands and knead lightly into a ball. Wrap and chill in the fridge for at least 2 hours until firm.

4. Preheat the oven to 150°C/Gas 2. Grease and base line a 25cm spring-release round cake tin (see page 212). Grease and flour the sides of the tin.

5. Divide the chilled dough in half; rewrap one half and return to the fridge. Coarsely grate the other half into the tin to cover the bottom evenly.

6. Carefully spoon on the cranberry sauce, leaving 1cm clear at the edge. Grate the remaining streusel dough evenly over the top. Bake in the oven for 1¼–1½ hours until pale but firm. Dust generously with icing sugar whilst still hot. Leave to cool in the tin, then unclip the tin, remove the cake and serve, cut into wedges.

VARIATION

REPLACE THE CRANBERRIES WITH NO-NEED-TO-SOAK APRICOTS AND THE JUICE OF 2 ORANGES. FOLLOW STEP 1 AS ABOVE, BUT SIMMER UNTIL ALL THE JUICE HAS EVAPORATED AND THE APRICOTS ARE SOFT. STIR IN 50G TOASTED FLAKED ALMONDS.

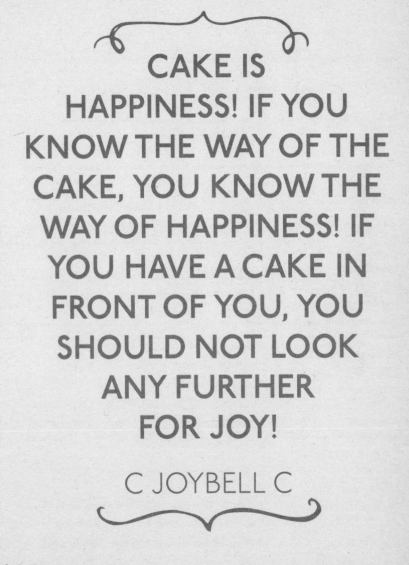

CAKE IS
HAPPINESS! IF YOU
KNOW THE WAY OF THE
CAKE, YOU KNOW THE
WAY OF HAPPINESS! IF
YOU HAVE A CAKE IN
FRONT OF YOU, YOU
SHOULD NOT LOOK
ANY FURTHER
FOR JOY!

C JOYBELL C

CHRISTMAS MORNING MUFFINS

MOIST MUFFINS BURSTING WITH CRANBERRIES MAKE A WONDERFUL START TO THE CELEBRATIONS!

MAKES 12

175g fresh cranberries
50g icing sugar, sifted
150g plain
  wholemeal flour
150g plain white flour
1 tbsp baking powder
1 tsp ground mixed
  spice
½ tsp salt
50g light
  muscovado sugar
1 egg
250ml milk
60ml vegetable oil

1. Halve the cranberries and place in a bowl with the icing sugar. Toss gently to mix.

2. Line a 12-cup muffin tin with paper cases or simply grease with butter. Sift together the white and wholemeal flour, baking powder, mixed spice, salt and muscovado sugar into a large bowl. Make a well in the centre.

3. Preheat the oven to 180°C/Gas 4.

4. Beat the egg with the milk and oil. Add to the dry ingredients and stir until just combined, then lightly and

DREAMY DELIGHTS

quickly stir in the cranberries. The mixture should look roughly mixed, with lumps and floury pockets.

5. Fill the muffin cups two-thirds full with the mixture. Bake in the oven for about 20 minutes or until well risen and golden brown.

6. Transfer the muffins to a wire rack to cool slightly. Serve whilst still warm.

HONEY AND YOGHURT MUFFINS

THIS AMERICAN-STYLE MUFFIN IS LIGHT, AIRY AND PERFECT SERVED WITH JUST A DOT OF BUTTER WHILE STILL WARM.

MAKES 12

225g plain white flour

1½ tsp baking powder

1 tsp bicarbonate of soda

a pinch of salt

¼ tsp ground mixed spice

¼ tsp ground nutmeg

50g medium oatmeal, plus extra for dusting

50g light muscovado sugar

50g unsalted butter

225g Greek-style yoghurt

1. Preheat the oven to 200°C/Gas 6. Line a 12-cup muffin tin with paper cases. Sift the flour, baking powder, bicarbonate of soda, salt, mixed spice and nutmeg into a bowl. Stir in the oatmeal and sugar.

2. Melt the butter and leave to cool slightly. Mix the yoghurt and milk together in a bowl, then beat in the egg, butter and honey. Pour over the dry ingredients and stir in quickly until only just blended; do not over-mix.

125ml milk
1 egg
4 tbsp runny honey

3. Divide the mixture equally between the paper cases. Sprinkle with oatmeal and bake for 17–20 minutes until well risen and just firm to the touch. Remove from the oven and leave in the tins for 5 minutes, then transfer to a wire rack. Serve warm or cold, with a little butter if desired.

VARIATION

FOR CHOCOLATE BANANA MUFFINS, OMIT THE HONEY, AND MASH 1 SMALL RIPE BANANA. MIX WITH 125G MELTED DARK CHOCOLATE AND ADD TO THE MUFFIN MIXTURE AFTER THE LIQUIDS, BLENDING UNTIL RIPPLED WITH COLOUR.

Espresso Cakes

THESE SMALL CAKES, RICHLY FLAVOURED YET DELICATELY PROPORTIONED, MAKE AN INTERESTING VARIATION ON A REGULAR COFFEE SPONGE.

MAKES 7

3 eggs

75g light or dark muscovado sugar

75g plain white flour

FOR THE MOCHA CUSTARD

15g chocolate-coated coffee beans

40g caster sugar

20g cornflour

2 egg yolks

½ tsp vanilla extract

1. Preheat the oven to 200°C/Gas 6. Grease and line a 33cm x 23cm Swiss roll tin (see page 213).

2. Put the eggs and sugar in a large heatproof bowl over a pan of simmering water and whisk until the mixture is thick enough to leave a trail on the surface when the whisk is lifted. Remove the bowl from the pan and whisk until cooled.

3. Sift the flour over the whisked mixture and fold in carefully, using a large metal spoon. Turn into the

200ml milk

90ml double cream

2 tbsp instant
espresso powder

TO ASSEMBLE

cocoa powder,
for dusting

90ml double cream

2 tsp instant espresso
powder

chocolate-coated
coffee beans,
chopped, to decorate

prepared tin, gently easing the mixture into the corners. Bake for 10–12 minutes until well risen and just firm. Turn out onto a clean sheet of greaseproof paper and peel away the lining paper.

4. To make the custard, finely chop the chocolate-coated coffee beans. Place the sugar, cornflour, egg yolks, vanilla extract and a little of the milk in a bowl and beat until smooth. Put the rest of the milk, the cream and espresso powder in a saucepan and bring to the boil. Pour over the custard, stirring until smooth. Return to the heat and cook, stirring, for 2–3 minutes until thickened. Stir in the chopped coffee beans. Transfer to a bowl and cover the surface with a piece of greaseproof paper to prevent a skin forming. Leave to cool.

5. Using a 6cm metal cutter, cut out 14 rounds from the sponge.

6. Spoon a little custard onto half of the rounds, then top with the remaining sponges. Whip the cream until just peaking and spoon a little on top of each cake. Sprinkle with the

NOTE

ESPRESSO COFFEE GIVES A STRONG FLAVOUR. USE A MILDER COFFEE IF PREFERRED.

espresso powder and decorate each cake with chopped chocolate-coated coffee beans. Chill until ready to serve. Dust generously with cocoa powder just before serving.

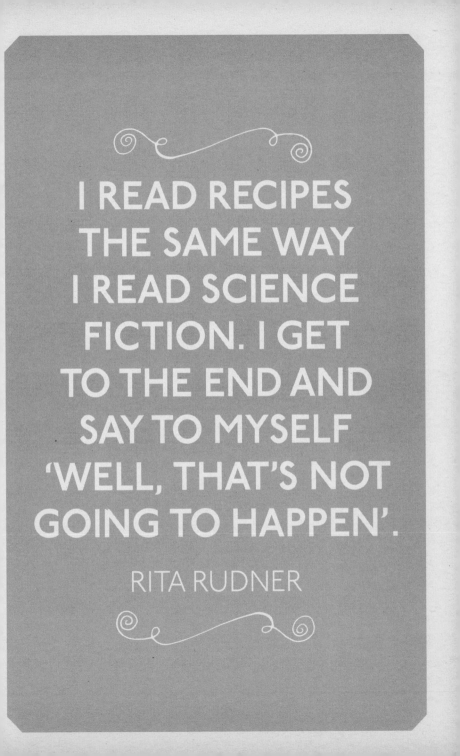

I READ RECIPES
THE SAME WAY
I READ SCIENCE
FICTION. I GET
TO THE END AND
SAY TO MYSELF
'WELL, THAT'S NOT
GOING TO HAPPEN'.

RITA RUDNER

Orange Curd and Hazelnut Meringue Cake

THIS IS A VERY IMPRESSIVE-LOOKING CAKE, WHICH COMBINES BEAUTIFULLY CHEWY, NUTTY MERINGUE WITH A SLIGHTLY SHARP CURD.

SERVES 6

125g blanched
  hazelnuts
4 large egg whites
250g golden caster
  sugar
½ tsp white vinegar
½ tsp vanilla extract

**FOR THE
ORANGE CURD**

2 eggs
225g caster sugar
zest of 1 orange
50ml orange juice
25ml lime juice
40g unsalted butter

1. First make the orange curd. Beat the eggs together in a heatproof bowl then add the sugar. Combine thoroughly then add all the other ingredients. Cook over a pan of simmering water, stirring constantly, until the curd coats the back of your spoon. Strain immediately into a jar and allow to thicken and cool before using.

2. Preheat the oven to 170°C/Gas 3. Grease and base line three 20cm round sandwich tins with non-stick baking parchment (see page 212).

FOR THE FILLING
400ml double cream

TO FINISH
1 tbsp icing sugar

3. Toast the hazelnuts in a dry frying pan until they start to turn a light golden brown. Allow to cool completely then grind to the consistency of fine breadcrumbs.

4. Whisk the egg whites to soft peaks, then gradually add the sugar, creating a stiff, glossy meringue. Add the vinegar and vanilla and whisk one last time. Stir in the hazelnuts.

5. Divide the meringue between the sandwich tins and use a palette knife to smooth down the top. Bake in the oven for 25 minutes, until the meringue is a golden brown, then remove from the oven and leave to cool in the tins.

6. Whisk the cream until fairly stiff, then lightly fold in the icing sugar.

7. To assemble the cake, place one layer of meringue on a plate and spread over half the cream, ensuring it goes right to the edges as you want it to spill over a little. Do the same with half of the orange curd. Add the second layer of meringue and use up the rest of the cream and curd, then place the final layer on top. Dust the finished cake with icing sugar.

Chocolate Mousse Cake

THE SUGAR-CRUSTED, CRACKED EXTERIOR
OF THIS CAKE RATHER BELIES THE SOFT,
SOUFFLÉ-TEXTURED CONSISTENCY WITHIN.
DURING COOKING IT RISES DRAMATICALLY,
THEN DEFLATES WHILE COOLING.

SERVES 8

225g dark chocolate
(at least 70% cocoa
solids)

125g unsalted butter

2 tbsp brandy

5 eggs, separated

125g caster sugar

1 tsp ground cinnamon

TO DECORATE

50g dark chocolate
(at least 70% cocoa
solids)

1. Preheat the oven to 160°C/Gas 3.
Grease and line a 23cm spring-release
round cake tin (see page 212).

2. Break up the chocolate and place
in a heatproof bowl over a pan of
simmering water (see page 218). Add
the butter and leave until melted.
Remove from the heat, add the brandy
and stir until smooth.

3. Place the egg yolks in a bowl
with 75g of the sugar. Whisk until
the mixture is pale and thick enough

125g strawberries
chocolate curls
(see page 219)
icing sugar, for dusting

to leave a trail on the surface when the whisk is lifted. Stir in the melted chocolate mixture.

4. In a separate bowl, whisk the egg whites until stiff. Gradually whisk in the remaining sugar, adding the cinnamon with the final addition of sugar. Using a large metal spoon, fold a quarter of the egg whites into the chocolate mixture to loosen it, then carefully fold in the remainder.

5. Turn the mixture into the prepared tin. Bake for 30–40 minutes until well risen and the centre feels just spongy when gently pressed. Leave to cool in the tin.

6. When cool, unclip the tin, peel off the paper and transfer the cake to a serving plate. For the decoration, break up the chocolate and melt in a heatproof bowl set over a pan of simmering water (see page 218). Dip the strawberries in the chocolate to half-coat (see page 219). Casually pile the chocolate curls and strawberries on top of the cake and lightly dust with icing sugar.

Almond and Chocolate Brittle Cake

LAYERS OF DARK AND CREAMY WHITE CHOCOLATE, SPECKLED WITH MILK CHOCOLATE CHIPS AND TOASTED ALMONDS.

MAKES ABOUT 24 PIECES

rice paper, for lining the tin

100g blanched almonds

200g dark chocolate (at least 70% cocoa solids)

200g white chocolate

finely pared zest of 1 small orange

2 tbsp Cointreau

50g milk chocolate, roughly chopped

1. Line the base and 1cm up the side of an 18cm round cake tin with rice paper (using the same technique as you would for lining a tin with greaseproof paper, see page 212).

2. Preheat the grill to medium and toast the almonds on a baking tray, turning occasionally, until evenly golden, then chop into large chunks.

3. Break up the dark chocolate and melt in a heatproof bowl set over a pan of simmering water (see page 218).

Spread half the melted chocolate over the base and lined sides of the prepared tin.

4. Melt the white chocolate in a separate bowl (as above) and allow to cool. Lightly stir the orange zest into the melted white chocolate, together with the liqueur. Stir in half the almonds and half the milk chocolate pieces.

5. Spoon the white chocolate mixture over the dark chocolate base, almost to the edge of the tin. Cover with the remaining melted dark chocolate. Immediately sprinkle with the rest of the nuts and the milk chocolate, pressing them down into the cake.

6. Leave in a cool place for at least 4 hours until set. Remove from the tin and break into chunks to serve.

NOTE

MAKE SURE THE WHITE CHOCOLATE IS COOL BEFORE ADDING THE MILK CHOCOLATE PIECES, OTHERWISE THE COLOURS WILL BLEND TOGETHER.

MINI COFFEE CUPS

THESE DELICATE CHOCOLATE CUPS CLEVERLY CONCEAL TWO COMPLEMENTARY LAYERS: ONE SMOOTH, WHITE AND CREAMY, THE OTHER FUDGE-LIKE AND FLAVOURED WITH COFFEE AND BRANDY.

MAKES 20

175g dark chocolate
(at least 70% cocoa
solids)

FOR THE FILLING

75g white chocolate
50ml double cream
75g dark chocolate
(at least 70% cocoa
solids)
2 tsp instant espresso
powder
1 tbsp brandy

TO DECORATE

40g white chocolate

1. Break up 125g of the dark chocolate and melt in a heatproof bowl over a pan of simmering water (see page 218). Separate twenty 3cm small foil or paper petit four cases. (Use double thickness paper cases to make the task of coating easier.)

2. Spoon a little chocolate into each case. Spread evenly over the base and sides using the back of a teaspoon. Invert on a tray lined with greaseproof paper. Leave in a cool place to set then turn the cases the right way up.

3. For the filling, break up the white chocolate and place in a small saucepan with the cream. Heat gently until the chocolate is melted. Remove from the heat and beat lightly. Allow the mixture to cool slightly then half-fill the chocolate cases.

4. Break up the dark chocolate and melt in a separate bowl (as above). Mix the instant espresso powder with I tablespoon of hot water. Add to the melted chocolate with the brandy and stir until smooth. Remove from the heat and cool slightly. Spoon over the white chocolate until only the rim of the chocolate case remains visible above the level of the filling.

5. Melt the remaining 50g dark chocolate for the cases in a bowl over a pan (as above). Melt the white chocolate for decoration in a separate bowl over a pan. Place the melted chocolates in separate piping bags.

6. Spread a little dark chocolate on one of the cups. Pipe a little white chocolate on top and immediately feather, by pulling a cocktail stick through the two. Repeat for the remaining cups. Keep in a cool place until ready to serve.

NOTE

MAKE SURE THE FILLING MIXTURES ARE NOT TOO WARM WHEN YOU FILL THE CHOCOLATE CASES, OTHERWISE THEY MAY MELT.

TELL ME WHAT YOU EAT, I'LL TELL YOU WHO YOU ARE.

JEAN ANTHELME
BRILLAT-SAVARIN

THE MORE YOU EAT, THE LESS FLAVOUR; THE LESS YOU EAT, THE MORE FLAVOUR.

CHINESE
PROVERB

MARGARITA DRIZZLE CAKE

IF YOU LIKE THE SLIGHTLY FIZZY, SHARP FLAVOURS OF A MARGARITA COCKTAIL, YOU WILL LOVE THIS.

SERVES 8

175g unsalted butter

175g caster sugar

zest of 2 limes

3 eggs

175g self-raising white flour

juice of I lime

I tbsp tequila

I tsp triple sec

FOR THE SYRUP

100g caster sugar

zest and juice of 2 limes

I tbsp tequila

I tsp triple sec

1. Preheat the oven to 180°C/Gas 4. Grease and base line a deep, loose-bottomed 20cm round cake tin (see page 212).

2. Beat together the butter, caster sugar and lime zest with an electric whisk until very light and fluffy. Mix in the eggs one at a time, alternating with tablespoons of self-raising flour, then lightly fold in the rest of the flour.

3. Stir in the lime juice, tequila and triple sec, then scrape the mixture into the prepared cake tin. Bake for 30–35 minutes until well risen, firm and golden brown.

TO DECORATE

a few very thin, long curls of lime zest

a pinch of sea salt (optional)

4. Make the syrup. Gently heat the caster sugar in a saucepan with the lime juice and zest. When the sugar has dissolved, leave on a very low heat for 3 minutes, then add the tequila and triple sec. Cook for a further minute, then strain into a jug.

5. While the cake is still hot, pierce all over with a skewer and pour over the syrup. Leave the cake until completely cool before turning out, as the syrup will make it fragile. Decorate with strips of lime zest and some crumbled sea salt, if desired.

LEMON CURD AND BLUEBERRY FAIRY CAKES

THESE FAIRY CAKES CONCEAL TWO SURPRISES
– JUICY BAKED BLUEBERRIES AND A CENTRE OF
LEMON CURD. THE TART BLUEBERRIES PERFECTLY
BALANCE OUT THE BUTTERY LEMON CURD.

MAKES 12

100g salted butter,
 softened

100g caster sugar

2 eggs, lightly beaten

finely grated zest
 of 1 lemon

100g self-raising
 white flour

125g blueberries

FOR THE TOPPING

3 tbsp lemon curd

1. Preheat the oven to 180°C/Gas 4.
Line a 12-cup muffin tin with paper
cases.

2. Cream the butter and sugar
together in a large bowl until light and
fluffy. Mix in the lightly beaten eggs,
then add the lemon zest. Sift the flour
over before folding in.

3. Spoon a tablespoon of mixture into
each paper case followed by a few
blueberries. Smooth the cake mixture

juice of ½ lemon

225g icing sugar

TO DECORATE

12 blueberries

over the top to cover the blueberries. Bake for 12–14 minutes or until the cakes are a light golden brown and springy to the touch. Remove from the oven and allow to cool.

4. Put the lemon curd into a piping bag with a fine nozzle and press the nozzle into the centre of each fairy cake. Squeeze firmly for a second to pump some lemon curd into each cake.

5. To make the icing mix the lemon juice with the icing sugar to make a thick, but spreadable icing. Spread icing onto each cake then immediately pipe a swirl of lemon curd onto the icing before it sets. Decorate each fairy cake with a blueberry.

NOTE

AS THESE CONTAIN FRESH FRUIT THEY WILL NOT KEEP FOR MORE THAN A COUPLE OF DAYS.

Hazelnut and Chocolate Meringue Cake

Tiers of subtly spiced meringue, laced with two-tone chocolate pieces, form a delicious case for lightly whipped cream and a hazelnut praline.

SERVES 10

125g skinned hazelnuts

5 egg whites

250g caster sugar

½ tsp ground mixed spice

75g white chocolate, chopped

75g dark chocolate (at least 70% cocoa solids), chopped

TO ASSEMBLE

75g skinned hazelnuts

125g caster sugar

1. Line two baking trays with non-stick baking parchment. Draw a 23cm circle onto one sheet, using a plate as a guide. On the other sheet, draw a 17.5cm circle. Turn the paper over. Preheat the oven to 140°C/Gas 1.

2. To make the meringue, lightly toast the hazelnuts in a dry frying pan, then chop roughly. Whisk the egg whites in a bowl until stiff. Gradually whisk in the sugar, a tablespoon at a time, whisking well between each addition until the

300ml double cream
I tbsp cocoa powder,
for dusting

meringue is stiff and very shiny.
Whisk in the spice with the last of the
sugar. Carefully fold in the chopped
hazelnuts and the white and dark
chocolate.

3. Spoon the meringue onto the
circles, then spread neatly into rounds.
Bake for about 1½ hours until dry
and the undersides are firm when
tapped. Turn the oven off and leave the
meringues to cool in the oven.

4. For the praline, lightly oil a baking
tray. Put the hazelnuts in a small
heavy-based pan with the sugar. Place
over a gentle heat, stirring until the
sugar melts. Continue cooking until the
mixture caramelizes to a rich golden
brown colour, then pour onto the
baking tray. Leave to cool and harden.

5. Place the praline in a polythene bag
and beat with a rolling pin until very
coarsely crushed.

6. Carefully transfer the largest
meringue round to a serving plate.
Whip the cream until softly peaking,
then spread over the meringue. Scatter
with the praline. Top with the smaller
meringue round and dust the surface
with cocoa powder just before serving.

NOTE

REMEMBER TO
SWITCH THE BAKING
SHEETS AROUND
HALFWAY THROUGH
COOKING THE
MERINGUE ROUNDS,
TO ENSURE AN
EVEN RESULT.

FRUITY
FAVOURITES

Holly Christmas Cake

THIS SIMPLE, ELEGANT CHRISTMAS CAKE IS TOPPED WITH PEAKED ROYAL ICING.

SERVES 12–14

- 75g glacé cherries, roughly chopped
- 400g raisins
- 175g currants
- 175g sultanas
- 50g chopped mixed peel
- 3 tbsp brandy
- 185g unsalted butter
- 185g dark muscovado sugar
- 3 eggs
- 225g plain white flour
- 1 tbsp black treacle
- 1 tsp each ground mixed spice, nutmeg and cinnamon

1. Preheat the oven to 140°C/Gas 1. Grease and line a deep 20cm round cake tin (see page 212). Place the cherries, raisins, currants, sultanas, peel and brandy in a bowl and stir lightly to combine.

2. In a separate bowl, cream the butter and sugar together until light and fluffy. Gradually beat in the eggs, adding a little of the flour to prevent curdling. Beat in the treacle. Sift the flour and spices over the mixture and fold in, then gently stir in the fruit and nuts.

75g Brazil nuts,
  roughly chopped
50g walnuts, roughly
  chopped

TO FINISH
3 tbsp apricot jam
700g marzipan
3 egg whites
1 tbsp glycerine
700g icing sugar

3. Turn the mixture into the prepared tin and level the surface. Bake for 3¼–3¾ hours until a skewer inserted in the centre comes out clean. Leave to cool in the tin. Turn out and wrap in a double thickness of foil. Store in a cool, dry place for up to 2 months.

4. To finish the cake, heat the apricot jam until melted, then press through a sieve into a bowl and stir in 1 tablespoon of hot water. Brush the cake with the glaze and cover with marzipan (see page 217).

5. To make the icing, mix the egg whites, glycerine and a little of the icing sugar in a bowl. Gradually beat in the remaining icing sugar until the icing is stiff and stands in soft peaks.

6. Use a generous half of the icing to cover the side of the cake, spreading with a palette knife to cover evenly. Trim off excess icing around the top. Leave to dry for 24 hours.

7. Spread the remaining icing over the top of the cake. Use a palette knife to pull up peaks, letting some overhang the side of the cake.

THE WORST
GIFT IS FRUITCAKE.
THERE IS ONLY ONE
FRUITCAKE IN THE
ENTIRE WORLD,
AND PEOPLE KEEP
SENDING IT TO
EACH OTHER.

JOHNNY CARSON

Hummingbird Cake

THIS FAMOUS AMERICAN CAKE HAILS FROM THE DEEP SOUTH. IT IS FABULOUSLY MOIST THANKS TO THE BANANA AND PINEAPPLE.

SERVES 8–10

250g plain white flour

1 tsp bicarbonate of soda

125g caster sugar

125g light muscovado sugar

3 large eggs

200ml sunflower oil

1 tsp vanilla extract

50g walnuts, finely chopped

3 large bananas, mashed

150g tinned pineapple, drained and finely chopped

1. Preheat the oven to 180°C/Gas 4. Grease and base line two deep 20cm round cake tins (see page 212). Sift together the plain flour and the bicarbonate of soda. Set aside.

2. In a food processor, beat together the sugars and eggs, then with the motor still running, gradually add all the oil and the vanilla extract. Fold in the flour, a little at a time, then add the walnuts, bananas and pineapple.

3. Divide the mixture between the prepared cake tins. Bake for 30–35 minutes until well risen and firm to

FOR THE CREAM CHEESE ICING

300g full-fat cream cheese

75g unsalted butter, softened

1 tsp orange blossom extract (optional)

1 tbsp orange juice

500g icing sugar

TO DECORATE

50g very finely chopped walnuts

the touch. Remove from the oven and leave to cool in their tins.

4. To make the cream cheese icing, beat together the cream cheese, butter, orange blossom extract, if using, and the orange juice until soft. Gradually sift in the icing sugar, folding in until well combined, then beat until the icing has increased dramatically in volume and is very fluffy. This should take around 5 minutes.

5. To assemble the cake, spread one of the cakes with some of the icing and place the other one on top. Cover the top and side of the cake with the icing, smoothing with a palette knife.

6. Decorate with the finely chopped walnuts. There are various ways to do this. You can cover either the top and/or the sides, or you can be more creative and cut out a stencil from a piece of card. If you can create a stencil in the shape of a hummingbird and infill it with finely ground walnuts, the cake looks stunning.

CELEBRATION CAKE

LUSTRE POWDER AND FRESH FLOWERS MAKE
THIS CAKE THE PERFECT CENTREPIECE FOR AN
ANNIVERSARY, WEDDING OR SPECIAL BIRTHDAY
GATHERING.

SERVES 40

150g glacé cherries

1.5kg mixed dried fruit

125g chopped
mixed peel

zest of 1 orange

4 tbsp Cointreau

375g unsalted butter,
softened

375g dark
muscovado sugar

5 eggs

450g plain white flour

1. Quarter the cherries and place in a bowl with the dried fruit, mixed peel and orange zest. Add the liqueur, stir lightly and leave to soak for several hours or overnight.

2. Grease and line a deep 25cm round cake tin (see page 212). Preheat the oven to 140°C/Gas 1.

3. Cream the butter and sugar together in a bowl until light and fluffy. Beat in the eggs, one at a time, adding a little of the flour with each egg to prevent curdling. Sift in the

TO DECORATE

3 tbsp apricot jam

900g marzipan

ivory food colouring

900g ready-to-roll
  sugarpaste

pearl lustre dusting
  powder

cocktail stick

selection of fresh
  flowers, such as
  gerberas, roses, etc.

remaining flour and fold to combine.
Add the soaked fruits and stir until
evenly mixed.

4. Scrape the cake mixture into the
prepared tin and bake for 3½–4 hours
or until a skewer inserted in the centre
comes out clean. Leave to cool in the
tin. When cool, turn out and wrap in a
double thickness of foil. Store in a cool
place for up to 2 months.

5. To decorate the cake, warm the
apricot jam and press through a sieve
into a bowl. Stir in 1 tablespoon of hot
water. Brush the cake with the glaze
and cover with the marzipan (see
page 217).

6. Knead a little ivory food colouring
into the sugarpaste. Use the icing to
cover the cake (see page 217). Roll
40 small balls from the sugarpaste
trimmings, the same size as the beads.
Leave to harden overnight.

7. The next day, once your sugarpaste
balls have hardened, moisten a little
dusting powder with water. Roll the
sugarpaste balls in the powder to give
them a subtle sheen.

8. Dip the end of a cocktail stick in a little water and use it to create indentations in the side of the cake at random intervals. Gently press the sugarpaste balls into the indentations to create a pattern.

9. Just before serving, arrange fresh, seasonal flowers on top of the cake for a special festive finish.

THE MOST DANGEROUS FOOD IS WEDDING CAKE.

JAMES THURBER

CINNAMON AND APPLE CRUMB CAKE

THE FLAVOURS OF APPLE AND CINNAMON ARE A MATCH MADE IN HEAVEN. THIS CAKE HAS A CRUMB TOPPING WHICH ADDS A DELICIOUS CRUNCH TO THE MOIST, SPICY SPONGE UNDERNEATH.

SERVES 8

250g self-raising white flour

1 tsp ground cinnamon

¼ tsp ground cloves

¼ tsp ground nutmeg

150g unsalted butter, softened

150g light muscovado sugar

2 large eggs

100ml milk

2 eating apples, peeled, cored and sliced into crescents

1. Preheat the oven to 180°C/Gas 4. Grease and base line a deep, loose-bottomed 20cm round cake tin (see page 212).

2. Sift together the flour and spices. Beat the butter with an electric whisk until soft, then add the sugar. Continue to beat together until very light and fluffy, then add the eggs, one by one, alternating with a tablespoon of the flour mixture.

FOR THE CRUMB TOPPING

25g unsalted butter

75g self-raising white flour

½ tsp ground cinnamon

a pinch of ground cloves

a pinch of ground nutmeg

75g Demerara sugar

50g finely chopped pecans

TO SERVE

crème fraîche

3. Fold in the rest of the flour and spices, then pour in the milk. You should have a fairly firm dropping consistency. Scrape the batter into the prepared tin and arrange the apple slices on top.

4. Make the crumb topping by rubbing the butter into the flour, spices and sugar. Stir in the pecans. Spread this mixture over the apples.

5. Bake for about an hour, until the cake is firm to the touch and a skewer inserted into the middle comes out clean. Leave to cool in the tin for 30 minutes, then turn out. This cake is delicious served with crème fraîche.

Almond and Apricot Roulade

Fresh ripe apricots and crème fraîche are encased inside an almond roulade and drizzled with Amaretto.

SERVES 8

25g flaked almonds
5 eggs, separated
150g caster sugar
1 tsp vanilla extract
125g marzipan, grated
3 tbsp plain white flour
3 tbsp Amaretto

FOR THE FILLING

caster sugar, for dusting
6 ripe apricots
300g crème fraîche

1. Preheat the oven to 180°C/Gas 4. Grease and line a 33cm x 23cm Swiss roll tin with non-stick baking parchment (see page 213). Scatter the flaked almonds evenly over the paper.

2. Whisk the egg yolks with 125g of the sugar until fluffy. Stir in the vanilla extract and grated marzipan. Sift the flour over the mixture, then fold in.

3. Whisk the egg whites in another bowl, until stiff. Gradually whisk in the remaining sugar. Using a large metal spoon, carefully fold a quarter of the egg whites into the almond mixture to loosen, then fold in the remainder.

4. Turn into the prepared tin and gently ease the mixture into the corners. Bake for about 20 minutes or until well risen and just firm to the touch. Remove from the oven and cover with a sheet of non-stick baking parchment and a damp tea towel. Leave to cool.

5. Remove the tea towel and invert the roulade (and paper) onto a baking tray. Peel off the lining paper. Sprinkle another piece of non-stick baking parchment with caster sugar and flip the roulade onto it. Drizzle with the Amaretto.

6. Halve and stone the apricots, then cut into small pieces. Spread the roulade with the crème fraîche and scatter with the apricots. Start at one of the narrow ends, roll up the roulade. Transfer to a plate and dust with caster sugar.

CRUMBLY APPLE AND CHEESE CAKE

THIS MOIST, CRUMBLY FRUITCAKE CONCEALS A LAYER OF TART CAERPHILLY CHEESE, WHICH PERFECTLY COMPLEMENTS THE SWEET TANG OF THE DESSERT APPLES.

SERVES 10

175g self-raising white flour

1 tsp baking powder

75g light muscovado sugar

50g raisins

50g sultanas

50g Brazil nuts, roughly chopped

575g dessert apples, peeled, cored and thinly sliced

2 eggs

90ml sunflower oil

1. Preheat the oven to 180°C/Gas 4. Grease a 5cm deep, 23cm round loose-based flan tin (see page 212).

2. Sift the flour and baking powder into a bowl. Stir in the sugar, raisins, sultanas, nuts and apples, and mix until evenly combined. Beat the eggs with the oil and add to the dry ingredients. Stir until the flour mixture is moistened and everything is evenly incorporated.

225g Caerphilly
cheese, crumbled

TO FINISH
I tbsp icing sugar,
for dusting

3. Turn half the mixture into the prepared tin and level the surface. Sprinkle the cheese over the surface, then cover with the remaining cake mixture. Roughly spread the mixture to the edges of the tin.

4. Bake for 50 minutes to I hour until golden and just firm. Leave to cool in the tin for 10 minutes, then transfer to a wire rack. Serve warm, dusted with icing sugar.

NOTE

DO NOT SMOOTH THE SECOND LAYER OF CAKE MIXTURE TOO NEATLY; A ROUGH SURFACE GIVES A MORE INTERESTING FINISH.

FRUITCAKE WITH GLACÉ FRUITS

AN IMPRESSIVE ARRANGEMENT OF COLOURFUL GLACÉ FRUITS PERFECTLY OFFSETS THIS CRUMBLY AND EXCEPTIONALLY MOIST FRUITCAKE.

SERVES 12

200g dried apple rings
300g mixed dried fruit
200g molasses sugar
175g unsalted butter
275ml cold black tea
350g self-raising white flour
1 tsp baking powder
1 tbsp ground mixed spice
1 egg
2 tbsp black treacle
100g glacé ginger pieces

1. Preheat the oven to 160°C/Gas 3. Grease and line a deep 23cm round cake tin (see page 212).

2. Roughly chop the apples and place in a saucepan with the mixed dried fruit, sugar, butter and tea. Bring to the boil, reduce the heat and simmer gently for 5 minutes. Remove from the heat and leave to cool completely.

3. Sift the flour, baking powder and mixed spice into a large bowl. Add the cooled fruit mixture, egg, treacle,

TO DECORATE

4 tbsp apricot jam

450g mixed glacé
fruits (pears,
plums, cherries,
pineapple, etc.)

ginger and liquid; beat well until the ingredients are evenly combined.

4. Turn the cake mixture into the prepared tin and level the surface. Bake for 1–1¼ hours, or until a skewer inserted in the centre comes out clean. Leave in the tin for 15 minutes, then transfer to a wire rack to cool.

5. To finish the cake, heat the apricot jam in a small saucepan until softened, then press through a sieve into a bowl. Brush a little of the warm apricot glaze over the cake.

6. Cut any larger pieces of glacé fruit into small wedges or slices. Arrange the fruits over the cake, then brush with the remaining glaze.

VARIATIONS

FOR A MORE EVERYDAY FRUITCAKE OMIT THE GLACÉ FRUIT TOPPING. INSTEAD, GENEROUSLY SPRINKLE THE TOP OF THE CAKE WITH DEMERARA SUGAR OR DECORATE WITH WHOLE BLANCHED ALMONDS BEFORE BAKING.

Strawberry Shortcake with Rose Chantilly Cream

NOT QUITE A BISCUIT, NOT QUITE A SPONGE, IT'S A SINGLE LAYER PILED HIGH WITH CREAM, STRAWBERRIES AND ROSE PETALS.

SERVES 8

75g ground almonds
225g unsalted butter
100g caster sugar
1 egg yolk
½ tsp rosewater
300g plain white flour
1 tsp baking powder

FOR THE TOPPING

200g double cream
1 tbsp icing sugar
a few drops of
  rosewater

1. Preheat the oven to 150°C/Gas 2. Grease a 24cm loose-bottomed round cake tin, then dust with flour. Sprinkle the base with a tablespoon of the ground almonds.

2. Beat the butter and sugar together until light and fluffy. Beat in the egg and the rosewater, then add the flour, baking powder and the rest of the ground almonds. You will have a very soft dough, which you can just about form into a ball.

400g strawberries
1 tbsp icing sugar
1 tsp lemon juice

TO DECORATE

a few small sprigs
  of mint
dried rose petals

3. Press the dough into the prepared tin as evenly as you can, then prick all over with a fork. Bake in the oven for 45 minutes, until it is a rich golden brown colour. Leave to cool in the tin and then turn out onto a serving plate – be careful, as the cake will be fragile.

4. Whip the cream until thick and quite firm, and stir in the sugar and rosewater. Hull and half the strawberries and toss in the icing sugar and lemon juice. Leave the sugar to dissolve, then strain.

5. Just before you are ready to serve (no sooner, as you don't want your shortcake to get soggy), pile the cream on top of the shortcake, and top with the strawberries. Sprinkle over some small sprigs of mint and rose petals.

Hinny Cakes with Sugared Blueberries

THESE MOIST TEATIME CAKES ARE SPICED WITH MACE AND CLOVES. ONCE COOKED, THEY'RE TOPPED WITH BLUEBERRIES AND CASTER SUGAR, THEN LIGHTLY GRILLED TO BRING OUT THE FULL FLAVOUR OF THE BERRIES.

MAKES 10

175g self-raising white flour
a pinch of salt
1 tsp baking powder
¼ tsp ground mace
¼ tsp ground cloves
75g unsalted butter
25g ground rice
25g caster sugar
90ml milk
2 tbsp sunflower oil

1. Sift the flour, salt, baking powder, mace and cloves into a bowl. Add 50g of the butter, cut into small pieces, and rub in using your fingertips until the mixture resembles fine breadcrumbs. Stir in the ground rice and sugar. Add the milk and mix to a fairly soft dough, using a round-bladed knife.

2. Turn the dough out onto a lightly floured surface and knead very lightly.

TO FINISH

225–350g blueberries
40g caster sugar
lightly whipped cream

Cut into 10 equal pieces. Using lightly floured hands, shape each piece into a small flat cake.

3. Melt 15g of the remaining butter with half the oil in a large heavy-based frying pan or griddle. Place half of the cakes in the pan and fry gently for 3–4 minutes until golden underneath. Turn the cakes over and cook for a further 3–4 minutes until cooked through. Transfer to a large baking tray. Melt the remaining butter with the oil and fry the rest of the cakes.

4. Preheat the grill to medium. Spoon the blueberries onto the cakes, piling them up slightly in the centre. Sprinkle with the sugar. Place under the grill for about 2 minutes, watching closely, until the blueberries are bubbling and the cake edges are lightly toasted. Serve immediately, with whipped cream.

NOTE

IT IS ESSENTIAL TO COOK THESE CAKES OVER A VERY GENTLE HEAT. A HIGH TEMPERATURE WILL OVERCOOK THE CRUSTS WHILE THE CENTRES REMAIN RAW.

Cinnamon Wafers
with Raspberries

FLAVOURFUL RASPBERRIES ARE LAYERED WITH
CREAM AND YOGHURT BETWEEN ROUNDS OF CRISP
HONEY AND CINNAMON WAFERS, THEN DUSTED
GENEROUSLY WITH ICING SUGAR.

SERVES 8

50g unsalted butter (at
  room temperature)

75g icing sugar

4 tbsp runny honey

75g plain white flour

1 tsp ground cinnamon

1 egg white, lightly
  beaten

FOR THE FILLING

300ml double cream

150ml Greek-style
  yoghurt

2 tbsp icing sugar

1. Preheat the oven to 220°C/Gas 7.
Line two large baking trays with
greaseproof paper.

2. Beat the butter in a bowl until very
soft, then beat in the icing sugar and
honey. Sift the flour and cinnamon
together and stir into the mixture with
the egg white to make a smooth batter.

3. Drop 4–6 heaped teaspoonfuls of
the mixture onto each baking tray,
spacing them well apart, and spread

2 tbsp framboise or
kirsch (optional)
350–450g raspberries

TO DECORATE
icing sugar, for dusting
mint sprigs

out to 7.5cm rounds using the back of
the spoon. Bake in the oven for
5–7 minutes until golden then carefully
lift off the baking sheet with a palette
knife and transfer to a wire rack to cool
and crisp. Use the remaining mixture
to make at least 24 wafers in all.

4. To make the filling, whip the cream
to soft peaks. Fold in the yoghurt,
sugar and liqueur, if using.

5. To assemble, layer up the wafers
in threes, sandwiching them together
with the cream and raspberries. Dust
generously with icing sugar and serve
at once, decorated with mint sprigs.

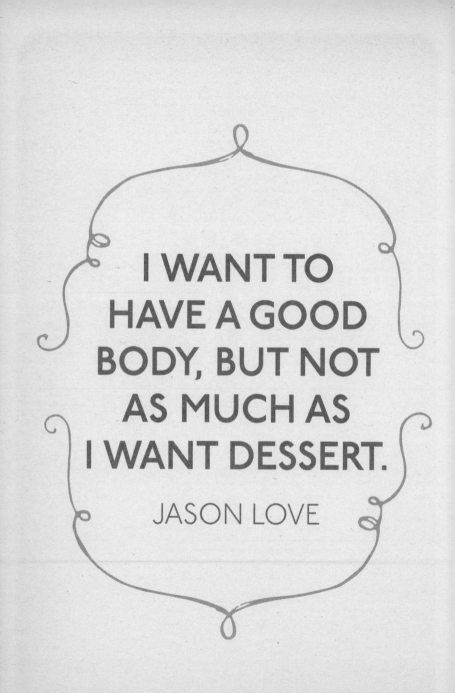

IF YOU'RE FEELING A LITTLE BIT DOWN, A LITTLE BIT OF KNEADING REALLY HELPS.

MARY BERRY

LAID-BACK LOAVES

STICKY GINGERBREAD

STICKY BLACK TREACLE AND SYRUPY STEM GINGER MAKE A PERFECT PARTNERSHIP IN THIS DELICIOUS ADAPTATION OF AN ALL-TIME FAVOURITE. GRATED COOKING APPLE IS ADDED FOR EXTRA MOISTURE.

SERVES 12

- I large cooking apple, about 225g
- I tbsp lemon juice
- 125g black treacle
- 125g golden syrup
- 175g molasses or dark muscovado sugar
- 175g unsalted butter
- 225g plain white flour
- 125g plain wholemeal flour
- I tsp ground mixed spice

I. Preheat the oven to 160°C/Gas 3. Grease and line a deep 18cm square cake tin (see page 212).

2. Peel, core and quarter the apple; drop in a bowl of water with the lemon juice added to prevent discolouration.

3. Put the treacle, syrup and sugar in a saucepan. Cut the butter into pieces and add to the pan. Heat gently until the butter melts; leave to cool slightly.

1½ tsp bicarbonate
of soda

2 eggs

150g stem ginger
pieces, thinly sliced,
plus 3 tbsp of syrup
from the jar

4. Sift the plain and wholemeal flour, spice and bicarbonate of soda into a bowl. Grate three-quarters of the apple into the bowl and toss lightly in the flour. Add the melted mixture, eggs and three-quarters of the ginger pieces. Beat well until thoroughly combined.

5. Turn the mixture into the prepared tin, spreading it into the corners. Using a potato peeler, pare the remaining apple into thin slices. Scatter the apple slices and remaining ginger pieces over the surface of the gingerbread and press down lightly into the mixture with the tip of a knife. Bake for 1 hour and 20 minutes until firm to touch. Leave to cool in the tin.

6. Turn out the cake and drizzle the ginger syrup over the surface.

> ### NOTE
> GINGERBREAD KEEPS WELL IN AN AIRTIGHT TIN FOR UP TO A WEEK. IT'S BEST STORED FOR SEVERAL DAYS BEFORE EATING.

MY WIFE DRESSES TO KILL. SHE COOKS THE SAME WAY.

HENNY YOUNGMAN

ALMOND, CHOCOLATE AND SWEET POTATO LOAF

THIS RECIPE USES PURÉED SWEET POTATO TO MOISTEN AND SUBTLY FLAVOUR THE CAKE.

SERVES 8–10

225g sweet potatoes, peeled and cut into chunks

125g soft baking spread

125g light muscovado sugar

1 tsp vanilla extract

2 eggs

160g self-raising white flour

15g cocoa powder

1 tsp ground mixed spice

½ tsp bicarbonate of soda

2 tbsp milk

1. Put the sweet potatoes in a pan of cold water, bring to the boil and cook for 15 minutes or until softened. Drain well, then mash with a potato masher.

2. Preheat the oven to 160°C/Gas 3. Grease a 1.5 litre loaf tin and line the base and long sides with a double thickness of greaseproof paper, allowing it to overhang the sides of the tin (see page 212).

3. Put the baking spread, sugar, vanilla extract and eggs in a bowl. Sift the flour, cocoa powder, mixed spice and

125g milk chocolate,
roughly chopped

75g flaked almonds,
lightly toasted

TO FINISH

1 tbsp icing sugar,
for dusting

bicarbonate of soda into the bowl.
Add the milk and beat well until
smooth and creamy.

4. Stir in the mashed sweet potato,
chopped chocolate and 50g of the
toasted almonds. Turn the mixture into
the prepared tin and level the surface.
Sprinkle with the remaining almonds.

5. Bake for about 1–1¼ hours until well
risen and just firm to touch. Leave in
the tin for 10 minutes, then transfer to
a wire rack to cool. Serve dusted with
icing sugar.

Pumpkin Teacake with Spiced Raisins

THIS IS AN OLD-FASHIONED TEACAKE, MADE MOIST BY THE ADDITION OF PUMPKIN. IT IS LOVELY STILL WARM FROM THE OVEN, ALTHOUGH YOU WILL NEED TO BE CAREFUL CUTTING IT AT THIS POINT AS IT WILL BE DIFFICULT TO SLICE.

SERVES 10–12

100g raisins
100ml hot tea
1 cinnamon stick
1 piece of mace
1 long strip of
  lemon zest
175g plain white flour
2 tsp baking powder
½ tsp bicarbonate
  of soda
¼ tsp freshly
  grated nutmeg

1. Put the raisins in a saucepan with the tea, cinnamon, mace and lemon zest. Bring to the boil and remove from the heat. Leave to infuse for at least 1 hour.

2. Preheat the oven to 170°C/Gas 3. Grease and line 1.5 litre loaf tin (see page 212). Sift together the flour, baking powder, bicarbonate of soda and nutmeg.

125g unsalted
   butter, melted
150g caster sugar
2 large eggs
200g cooked and
   mashed pumpkin

3. In a large bowl, beat together the butter and sugar. Add the eggs, followed by the pumpkin and the drained raisins. Finally, gradually incorporate the flour mixture until everything is very well combined.

4. Scrape the batter into the prepared loaf tin and bake in the oven for about 1 hour, until golden brown and a skewer inserted into the middle comes out clean. Allow to cool in the tin before turning out.

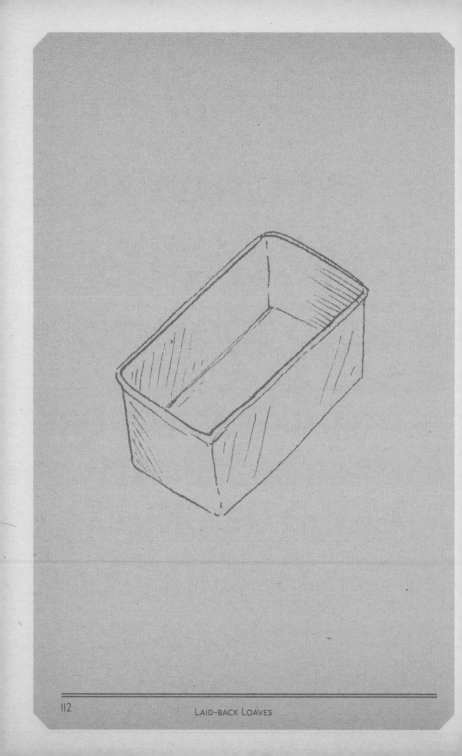

YOU HAVE TO EAT TO COOK. YOU CAN'T BE A GOOD COOK AND BE A NON-EATER. I THINK EATING IS THE SECRET TO GOOD COOKING.

JULIA CHILD

APPLE, SULTANA
AND CIDER SLICES

THIS SIMPLE SPONGE IS RICHLY FILLED WITH SWEET,
FRAGRANT DESSERT APPLES AND SULTANAS AND
BAKED ON A PUFF PASTRY BASE.

MAKES 12

225g ready-made puff
pastry (or 1/3 of the
recipe on page 214)

3 dessert apples

1 tbsp lemon juice

175g unsalted butter,
softened

175g caster sugar

125g self-raising
white flour

75g self-raising
wholemeal flour

½ tsp baking powder

3 eggs

1. Preheat the oven to 200°C/Gas 6.
Lightly dampen a large baking tray.
Roll out the pastry thinly on a lightly
floured surface to a 28cm square and
place on the baking tray. Prick the
surface all over with a fork and bake
for 10 minutes until risen. Lower the
oven temperature to 180°C/Gas 4.

2. Lightly grease a 23cm square
shallow baking tin. Cut the pastry to
fit the base of the tin, then carefully
press into position.

3 tbsp medium
  dry cider
50g sultanas
2 tsp icing sugar

TO FINISH
icing sugar, for dusting

3. Peel, core and slice one of the apples. Place in a bowl of water with I teaspoon of the lemon juice. Core and slice the remaining apples (do not peel them) and place in a separate bowl with the remaining lemon juice.

4. Cream the butter and sugar together in a bowl until pale and creamy. Sift the flours and baking powder into a bowl. Add the eggs and cider and beat well until smooth. Drain the peeled apple slices and stir into the mixture with the sultanas. Spoon over the pastry and level the surface.

5. Drain the unpeeled apple slices and arrange over the filling. Dust with the icing sugar and bake for 45–50 minutes until just firm. Leave to cool in the tin for 15 minutes.

6. Dust the cake with more icing sugar and serve warm, cut into squares.

Date and Banana Loaf

THIS HOMELY TEA BREAD HAS A BEAUTIFULLY
MOIST TEXTURE AND A DISTINCTIVE BANANA
TASTE, WITH A SLIGHT TANG. LAYERS OF PURÉED
DATES ADD EXTRA DEPTH OF FLAVOUR.

SERVES 8–10

250g stoned
  dried dates

zest and juice
  of 1 lemon

2 ripe bananas

175g unsalted
  butter, softened

175g caster sugar

2 eggs

225g self-raising
  white flour

½ tsp baking powder

1. Preheat the oven to 160°C/Gas 3.
Grease and line a 1.2 litre loaf tin (see
page 212).

2. Set aside 4 dates. Place the
remainder in a small heavy-based
saucepan and add the lemon zest and
juice, and 90ml water. Bring to the boil,
reduce the heat and simmer gently
for 5 minutes until the dates are soft
and pulpy. Purée the mixture in a food
processor or blender until smooth, or
mash together in a bowl with a fork.

3. Mash the bananas until completely smooth. Cream the butter and sugar together in a bowl until light and fluffy. Add the banana purée and the eggs. Sift the flour and baking powder into the bowl and beat until thoroughly combined.

4. Spoon one-third of the banana mixture into the prepared loaf tin and level the surface. Spread half of the date purée over the surface. Repeat these layers, then cover with the remaining banana mixture.

5. Cut the reserved dates into thin lengths and scatter them over the surface. Bake for 1–1¼ hours until well risen and firm to the touch. Leave in the tin for 15 minutes, then transfer to a wire rack to cool. Store in an airtight container for up to a week.

TIP

THE DATE PURÉE NEEDS TO BE SIMILAR IN CONSISTENCY TO THE BANANA MIXTURE. IF IT SEEMS TOO THICK, BEAT IN A LITTLE WATER.

Honey, Vanilla and Blueberry Loaf

The pairing of honey and vanilla is one of the most comforting of combinations.

SERVES 8–10

250g unsalted butter, softened

150g caster sugar

75g runny honey

3 large eggs

300g self-raising white flour

1 tsp vanilla extract

1 tbsp milk

200g blueberries

2 tbsp caster sugar

1. Preheat the oven to 170°C/Gas 3. Grease and line 1.5 litre loaf tin (see page 212).

2. Beat the butter until very soft and then add the sugar and honey. Cream together until the mixture is very soft, light and fluffy.

3. Mix in the eggs one at a time, folding in a tablespoon of the flour after each addition. Gently fold in the rest of the flour, then mix in the vanilla extract and milk. The batter will be slightly firmer than a dropping consistency.

4. Scrape half the batter into the prepared loaf tin. Fold half the blueberries through the remaining batter and spoon this on top. Scatter the rest of the blueberries over the top of the cake and sprinkle over the caster sugar.

5. Bake for about 1 hour, or until a skewer inserted into the middle comes out clean. Leave to cool in its tin.

CHERRY STREUSEL SLICE

CRUMBLY, MILDLY SPICED AND PLEASANTLY SWEET, THIS MOUTH-WATERING CAKE IS REMINISCENT OF A TRADITIONAL FRUIT CRUMBLE. SERVE SLICED, WITH SPOONFULS OF LIGHTLY WHIPPED CREAM AS A TEATIME TREAT.

SERVES 8

2 x 425g tins pitted
  black or red cherries

2 tsp cornflour

I tsp vanilla extract

250g self-raising
  white flour

I tsp ground cinnamon

zest of ½ lemon

175g unsalted butter

165g caster sugar

50g ground almonds

I egg

I. Drain the cherries, reserving 90ml of the juice. Blend a little of the juice with the cornflour in a small pan. Add the remaining juice and vanilla extract and bring to the boil, stirring. Add the cherries and cook, stirring, for a further minute until thickly coated in the syrup. Leave to cool.

2. Grease a 1.5 litre loaf tin and line the base and long sides with a double thickness of greaseproof paper, allowing it to overhang the sides of the tin (see page 212). Preheat the oven to 180°C/Gas 4.

3. Place the flour, cinnamon and lemon zest in a food processor. Add the butter, cut into small pieces, and work until the mixture starts to cling together. Add the sugar and ground almonds, and process briefly until the mixture resembles a coarse crumble. (Alternatively rub the butter into the flour, cinnamon and lemon zest using your fingertips, then stir in the sugar and ground almonds.) Weigh 150g of the crumble and set aside for the topping. Add the egg to the remaining mixture and mix to a fairly soft paste.

4. Use half the paste to thickly line the base of the prepared tin. Roll out the remainder and cut into 2.5cm-wide strips. Use these to line the sides of the tin, pressing them to fit around the corners and base, eliminating the joins.

5. Spoon the cherry filling into the centre and sprinkle evenly with the reserved crumble. Bake for 40–45 minutes until the topping is pale golden. Leave in the tin to cool.

6. Loosen the edges at the end of the tin, then carefully lift the cake out, using the greaseproof paper. Serve dusted with icing sugar.

YOU DON'T COME INTO COOKING TO GET RICH.

GORDON RAMSAY

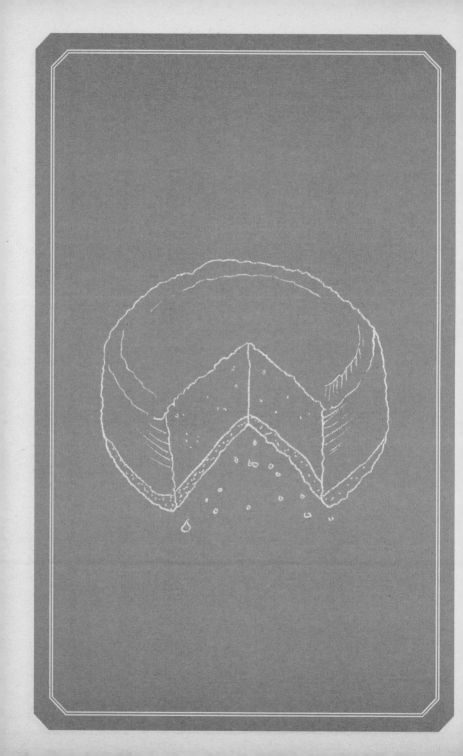

PEACEFUL PUDDINGS

Almond and Amaretti Cheesecake

A LIGHT, CREAMY CHEESECAKE MIXTURE IS ENCASED IN A CRUMBLY, CRUNCHY ALMOND CASE AND TOPPED WITH CRUSHED AMARETTI BISCUITS. MAKE THE CHEESECAKE A DAY BEFORE YOU NEED IT – THE TEXTURE IMPROVES ON KEEPING.

SERVES 8

75g unsalted butter
125g digestive biscuits
25g blanched almonds

FOR THE FILLING

125g mascarpone cheese
125g ricotta cheese
50g caster sugar
2 eggs, separated
½ tsp vanilla extract

1. Preheat the oven to 150°C/Gas 2. Grease and line a 20cm loose-based or spring-release round cake tin (see page 212). Melt the butter in a small pan. Meanwhile, whizz the biscuits and almonds in a food processor, or crush the biscuits using a rolling pin and chop the almonds finely, then mix into the butter.

1 tbsp cornflour
100ml crème fraîche
50g amaretti biscuits

FOR THE COMPÔTE
4 ripe nectarines
150ml white wine
75g caster sugar
1 vanilla pod

2. Spread the biscuit mixture over the base and about 1cm up the side of the tin, pressing it firmly with the back of a spoon. Set aside.

3. Place the mascarpone and ricotta cheeses in a large bowl and beat together well. Add the sugar, egg yolks, vanilla extract and cornflour and beat again, then fold in the crème fraîche. Whisk the egg whites to soft peaks. Stir one-third of the egg whites into the cheesecake mixture, then carefully fold in the rest.

4. Pour the mixture into the tin. Crumble the amaretti biscuit into chunky crumbs and scatter over the top. Bake in the oven for 1½ hours until just firm to the touch. Turn off the heat and leave the cheesecake to cool in the oven.

5. Meanwhile, make the nectarine compôte. Halve the nectarines, remove the stones, then cut into quarters and place in a saucepan with the wine, sugar, vanilla pod and 150ml water. Bring slowly to the boil, then reduce the heat, cover and simmer very gently for about 5 minutes until the nectarines are just tender. Allow to cool, then discard the vanilla pod and chill in the fridge for several hours.

6. Serve the cheesecake, cut into wedges, with the compôte.

RECIPE: A SERIES OF STEP-BY-STEP INSTRUCTIONS FOR PREPARING INGREDIENTS YOU FORGOT TO BUY, IN UTENSILS YOU DON'T OWN, TO MAKE A DISH THE DOG WOULDN'T EAT.

ANON

Chocolate, Walnut and Maple Pudding

THESE PRETTY INDIVIDUAL PUDDINGS ARE MADE FROM A WHISKED MIXTURE OF EGGS, COCOA POWDER, WALNUTS AND GROUND ALMONDS – RESULTING IN A LIGHT, SOUFFLÉ-LIKE TEXTURE.

SERVES 8

150g unsalted butter, softened

175g light muscovado sugar

¼ tsp ground nutmeg

25g plain white flour

4 tbsp cocoa powder

5 eggs, separated

125g ground almonds

50g breadcrumbs

50g shelled walnuts, chopped

1. Preheat the oven to 180°C/Gas 4. Grease 8 individual pudding basins and line the bases with greaseproof paper.

2. In a bowl, cream the butter with 50g of the sugar and the nutmeg until light and fluffy. Sift the flour and cocoa powder into the bowl. Add the egg yolks, ground almonds, breadcrumbs and nuts and stir until just combined.

3. Whisk the egg whites until stiff. Gradually whisk in the remaining

TO SERVE

crème fraîche

maple syrup

extra chopped
   walnuts, for
   sprinkling

sugar. Fold a quarter into the chocolate mixture, to lighten it, using a large metal spoon. Carefully fold in the remaining egg whites.

4. Spoon the mixture into the prepared basins, filling them no more than two-thirds full.

5. Stand the pudding basins in a roasting tin and pour in sufficient boiling water to give a 1cm depth. Cover the tin completely with foil and bake for 30 minutes or until the puddings feel firm.

6. Loosen the edges of the puddings with a knife and turn out onto warmed serving places. Put a spoonful of crème fraîche beside each pudding. Drizzle with maple syrup and sprinkle with chopped walnuts.

SUMMER PUDDING

THIS QUINTESSENTIAL BRITISH PUDDING NEEDS
NOTHING MORE THAN A DOLLOP OF CREAM. IT'S
EXTREMELY EASY TO MAKE AND – LIKE ALL GREAT
DINNER-PARTY PUDDINGS – IS MADE THE NIGHT
BEFORE, READY TO TURN OUT AND SERVE WHEN
REQUIRED.

SERVES 6–8

450g raspberries

225g redcurrants

225g blackcurrants

75g caster sugar

8 large slices white bread, 0.5m thick, crusts removed (see note)

1. Put the raspberries in a saucepan with the redcurrants, blackcurrants, sugar and 3 tablespoons of water. Bring to a gentle simmer over a low heat, then cook gently for 3–4 minutes until the juices begin to run. Remove from the heat and set aside.

2. Cut a round of bread from one of the slices to fit the base of a 1.5 litre pudding basin. Cut the remaining slices in half lengthways.

TO DECORATE

sprigs of redcurrants
lemon balm or
  mint leaves

TO SERVE

double cream

3. Arrange the bread slices around the side of the pudding basin, overlapping them slightly at the bottom, so they fit neatly and tightly together. Position the round of bread to cover the hole in the middle.

4. Spoon about 100ml of the fruit juice into a jug and set aside. Spoon the remaining fruit and its juice into the bread-lined pudding basin. Cover completely with the remaining bread slices, trimming them to fit as necessary.

5. Cover the pudding with a saucer that just fits inside the top of the pudding basin, then set a 2kg weight on the saucer (or use a couple of unopened cans from the store cupboard). Chill the pudding in the fridge overnight.

6. To serve the pudding, remove the weight and saucer and invert a serving plate over the pudding basin. Hold the two firmly together and turn them over. Give them a firm shake (up and down, rather than side to side), then lift off the pudding basin.

NOTE

CHOOSE A GOOD QUALITY CLOSE-TEXTURED LARGE WHITE LOAF, PREFERABLY ONE-DAY OLD.

7. Spoon the reserved juice over the pudding and decorate with redcurrant sprigs and lemon balm or mint sprigs. Serve, cut into wedges, with plenty of cream.

COOKING REQUIRES CONFIDENT GUESSWORK AND IMPROVISATION – EXPERIMENTATION AND SUBSTITUTION, DEALING WITH FAILURE AND UNCERTAINTY IN A CREATIVE WAY.

PAUL THEROUX

NEW YORK CHEESECAKE

THIS IS A CLASSIC NEW YORK CHEESECAKE, WHICH IS BAKED IN THE OVEN. THE TEXTURE IMPROVES INORDINATELY IF THE CHEESECAKE IS CHILLED OVERNIGHT IN THE FRIDGE.

SERVES 8–10

250g digestive biscuits
150g unsalted butter
1 tsp ground cinnamon

FOR THE FILLING

600g full-fat cream cheese
200g soft light brown sugar
3 eggs
1 egg yolk
150g sour cream
1 tsp vanilla extract
zest of 1 lemon

1. Whizz the biscuits in a food processor, or crush them using a rolling pin. Melt the butter in a saucepan. Remove from the heat, add the biscuit crumbs and the cinnamon and stir until combined. Press into a 20cm spring-release round cake tin. Put in the fridge to set for about 1 hour.

2. Preheat the oven to 180°C/Gas 4. Using an electric mixer beat the cream cheese until smooth. Continue to beat the mixture and add the sugar and

FOR THE TOPPING

150ml Marsala wine

juice of ½ lemon

75g caster sugar

50g raisins

then the eggs and egg yolk one by one. Slowly spoon in the sour cream, then add the vanilla extract and the lemon zest. Smooth the mixture over the biscuit base.

3. Cover the outside and base of the tin with a layer of foil. Put the tin in a large roasting tin and pour boiling water around it, so it comes about halfway up the side of the cake tin. Cook for about 50 minutes. The cheesecake should feel set, but with a bit of a wobble. Remove from the oven and leave to cool. Chill in the fridge overnight.

4. Meanwhile, make the raisin syrup topping. Put all the ingredients in a saucepan and simmer until the syrup has reduced a little. Allow to cool and chill in the fridge overnight. Serve the cheesecake with the raisin syrup drizzled over the top.

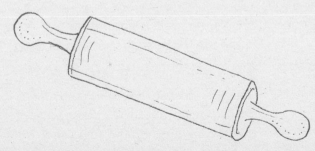

Bread and Butter Pudding

LIGHT AND FLAKY CROISSANTS REPLACE THE
USUAL BREAD IN THIS TRADITIONAL PUDDING.
SOAK THE SULTANAS IN A LITTLE BRANDY TO
PLUMP THEM UP IF YOU LIKE.

SERVES 6

4 large croissants
(see note)

75g unsalted butter (at
room temperature)

50g sultanas

FOR THE CUSTARD

300ml milk (at room
temperature)

300ml double
cream (at room
temperature)

I vanilla pod, split

6 egg yolks

1. Preheat the oven to 180°C/Gas 4.
Grease a 1.7 litre shallow baking dish.

2. Slice the croissants thickly, then
spread with the butter. Arrange the
croissant slices, butter-side up and
overlapping, in the prepared dish,
scattering in the sultanas as you go.

3. To make the custard, pour the milk
and cream into a saucepan. Add the
vanilla pod and place over a very low
heat for about 5 minutes until the

125g caster sugar

TO FINISH

1 tbsp icing sugar,
  for dusting

double cream

mixture is almost boiling and well
flavoured with vanilla.

4. Meanwhile, in a large bowl, whisk
together the egg yolks and caster
sugar until light and foamy. Strain the
flavoured milk onto the egg mixture,
whisking all the time.

5. Pour the egg mixture evenly over
the croissants. Place the dish in a large
roasting tin and pour enough boiling
water into the tin to come halfway up
the sides of the dish. Bake in the oven
for 45–50 minutes until the custard
is softly set and the top is crisp and
golden brown.

6. Remove from the oven and leave
the pudding in the bain-marie until just
warm. Dust with the icing sugar and
serve with cream.

NOTE

THE CROISSANTS ARE
BETTER USED WHEN
SLIGHTLY STALE.
LEAVE THEM IN A
COOL PLACE FOR
A DAY OR TWO, TO
DRY AND FIRM UP
BEFORE SLICING.

Chocolate Bread and Butter Pudding

THIS RECIPE HAS ALL THE COMFORTING QUALITIES OF A TRADITIONAL BREAD AND BUTTER PUDDING. THE BONUS HERE IS THE GENEROUS POCKETS OF DARK, GOOEY CHOCOLATE SAUCE MELTING INTO THE SPICED VANILLA CUSTARD. IRRESISTIBLE!

SERVES 6

200g dark chocolate (at least 70% cocoa solids)

75g unsalted butter

225g fruited loaf or light tea bread

1 tsp vanilla extract

½ tsp ground cinnamon

3 eggs

25g caster sugar

600ml milk

1. Lightly grease the sides of a 1.7 litre ovenproof dish. Break up the chocolate and put in a heatproof bowl set over a pan of simmering water. Add 25g of the butter and leave until melted. Stir lightly.

2. Cut the fruited bread into thin slices and arrange a third of the slices, overlapping in the prepared dish. Spread with half the chocolate sauce. Arrange half the remaining bread in

cocoa powder and icing sugar, for dusting

the dish and spread with the remaining sauce. Finally arrange the last of the bread slices in the dish.

3. Melt the remaining butter. Remove from the heat and stir in the vanilla extract, cinnamon, eggs, sugar and milk. Beat thoroughly, then pour over the bread. Leave to stand for 1 hour until the bread has softened. Preheat the oven to 180°C/Gas 4.

4. Bake the pudding in the oven for 45–55 minutes until the custard has set and the bread is deep golden brown. Leave to stand for 5 minutes. Dust with cocoa powder and icing sugar just before serving.

NOTE

USE A TEA BREAD THAT'S LIGHTLY DOTTED WITH FRUITS, OTHERWISE THE PUDDING WILL BE TOO HEAVY.

ALL SORROWS ARE LESS WITH BREAD.

CERVANTES

WHEN BAKING, FOLLOW DIRECTIONS. WHEN COOKING, GO BY YOUR OWN TASTE.

LAIKO BAHRS

Spiced Raisin Puddings with Demerara Lemon Sauce

FEW OF US WITH A PASSION FOR FOOD CAN RESIST THE TEMPTATION OF A HOT, STEAMING BRITISH PUDDING AND THIS ONE WON'T DISAPPOINT.

MAKES 8

15g preserved stem ginger in syrup

175g unsalted butter, softened

175g caster sugar

3 eggs, lightly beaten

225g self-raising white flour

1½ tsp baking powder

1 tsp ground mixed spice

½ tsp ground cinnamon

75g raisins

a little milk

1. Preheat the oven to 180°C/Gas 4. Lightly grease the base and sides of 8 individual 185ml metal pudding basins. Chop the ginger into tiny pieces.

2. In a bowl, cream together the butter and sugar until light and fluffy. Add the eggs, a little at a time, beating well after each addition, and adding a little of the flour to prevent curdling.

3. Sift the remaining flour, baking powder and the spices into the bowl.

FOR THE SAUCE

75g unsalted butter

175g Demerara sugar

zest and juice of
  2 small lemons

TO SERVE

double cream or
  crème fraîche

Add the raisins and chopped ginger and gradually fold in, using a large metal spoon. Stir in sufficient milk to give a soft, dropping consistency.

4. Divide the mixture among the prepared tins and level the surfaces. Stand in a roasting tin and pour boiling water around the tins to a depth of 1cm. Cover the roasting tin with foil. Bake for 40–45 minutes until the sponges have risen and feel firm to the touch.

5. Meanwhile, make the sauce. Melt the butter in a small saucepan. Add the sugar and heat gently for 2–3 minutes until bubbling. Add the lemon zest and juice and cook gently to make a buttery syrup.

6. Loosen the edges of the puddings with a knife, then invert onto warmed serving plates. Pour a little sauce over each one and serve with cream or crème fraîche.

Apple Bramble Pudding

BRAMLEY APPLES, BLACKBERRIES AND RASPBERRIES
ARE COOKED IN A SYRUPY BUTTER, THEN LAYERED
WITH SOFT BREAD AND BAKED TO A GOLDEN
CRUST. SERVE WITH CREAMY CUSTARD.

SERVES 6

125g unsalted butter

75g Demerara sugar

700g cooking apples

2 tbsp lemon juice

350g blackberries

225g raspberries

125g redcurrants
or blackcurrants

1 tbsp oil

6 slices traditional
white loaf, crusts
removed

a little Demerara sugar,
for sprinkling

1. Preheat the oven to 200°C/Gas 6.
Lightly grease a 1.7 litre ovenproof dish.
Melt 50g of the butter in a large pan.
Add the sugar and stir until beginning
to dissolve.

2. Peel, core and thickly slice the
apples and add to the pan. Cook gently,
stirring frequently, for 5 minutes.
Add the lemon juice, blackberries,
raspberries and redcurrants or
blackcurrants; toss lightly to combine.

3. Spoon half the fruit mixture into
the base of the ovenproof dish. Melt

the remaining butter in a frying pan with the oil, add half of the bread slices and fry until beginning to brown on the underside. Remove with a fish slice and lay the slices, browned sides uppermost, over the fruits in the dish. (Reserve the butter and oil.)

4. Spread the rest of the fruits and juices over the bread. Cut the remaining bread into triangles and arrange over the fruit in the dish. Brush liberally with the reserved butter and oil, then sprinkle with Demerara sugar. Bake for about 25 minutes until the bread topping is deep golden.

VARIATIONS

VIRTUALLY ANY COMBINATION OF SOFT FRUITS CAN BE USED IN THIS PUDDING, BUT AVOID TOO MANY BLACKCURRANTS AS THEIR FLAVOUR WILL DOMINATE.

THE BEST COOKING IS THAT WHICH TAKES INTO ACCOUNT THE PRODUCTS OF THE SEASON.

AUGUSTE ESCOFFIER

ALWAYS START OUT WITH A LARGER POT THAN WHAT YOU THINK YOU NEED.

JULIA CHILD

Sticky Date and Orange Pudding

FLAVOURED WITH ORANGES, DATES AND FLECKS OF WHITE CHOCOLATE, THE LIGHT-TEXTURED SPONGY PUDDING IS TOPPED WITH AN INDULGENT TOFFEE SAUCE. SERVE WITH CUSTARD OR POURING CREAM.

SERVES 6

175g stoned dates, roughly chopped

150ml fresh orange juice

75g unsalted butter, softened

150g light muscovado sugar

2 eggs

150g self-raising white flour

25g cocoa powder

½ tsp bicarbonate of soda

1. Butter a 1.4 litre pudding basin and line the base with a circle of greaseproof paper. Place the dates in a saucepan with the orange juice. Bring to the boil, reduce the heat and simmer gently for 5 minutes. Leave to cool while preparing the pudding.

2. Put the butter, sugar and eggs in a large bowl. Sift the flour, cocoa powder and bicarbonate of soda into the bowl and beat well until evenly combined.

zest of I orange

50g white chocolate, roughly chopped

FOR THE SAUCE

125g light muscovado sugar

75g unsalted butter

4 tbsp double cream

I tbsp lemon juice

TO SERVE

homemade custard (see page 216) or pouring cream

3. Using a slotted spoon, remove and set aside one-third of the date pieces from the saucepan. Add the remaining dates and orange juice to the pudding mixture with the orange zest and chopped chocolate. Stir well, then turn into the prepared basin.

4. Cover the basin with a double thickness of greaseproof paper and sheet of foil. Secure under the rim with string. Place in a steamer and add boiling water. Cover and steam for 2 hours. Top up with more boiling water as necessary during cooking.

5. Meanwhile, make the sauce. Put the sugar, butter and cream in a small pan. Heat gently until the sugar dissolves, then stir in the reserved dates and lemon juice. Boil for I minute.

6. Remove the pudding from steamer and invert onto a serving plate. Pour toffee sauce over the pudding to coat evenly. Serve any remaining sauce in a separate jug, along with custard or pouring cream.

NOTE

IF YOU DON'T HAVE A STEAMER, REST THE PUDDING BASIN ON AN UPTURNED OLD SAUCER IN A LARGE SAUCEPAN. POUR SUFFICIENT BOILING WATER INTO THE PAN TO COME HALFWAY UP THE SIDES OF THE BASIN.

CHRISTMAS PUDDING

A RICH AND STICKY FIGGY PUDDING PACKED WITH DRIED FRUITS PLUMPED UP WITH PORTER OR STOUT AND BRANDY. THE PUDDING IS KEPT MOIST WITH BUTTER INSTEAD OF SUET.

MAKES 2 PUDDINGS; EACH SERVES 8–10

250g dried mixed fruit
125g dried dates
225g sultanas
225g seedless raisins
150ml porter
  or sweet stout
4 tbsp brandy, dark
  rum or Armagnac
zest and juice of
  1 lemon
zest and juice
  of 1 orange
125g ready-to-eat
  dried figs

1. Place the mixed fruit, dates, sultanas and raisins in a shallow bowl and pour over the porter and brandy. Add the lemon and orange juice. Stir well, cover and leave to soak overnight, stirring occasionally.

2. The next day, drain the soaked fruit, reserving any juices and discarding any stones. Roughly chop the fruit, figs and ginger, and place in a large mixing bowl.

3. Stir in the almonds, breadcrumbs, sugar and spices. Grate the butter and fold into the mixture. Beat the eggs

125g preserved
  stem ginger

225g whole
  unblanched almonds

225g fresh brown
  breadcrumbs

225g dark muscovado
  sugar

1 tsp grated nutmeg

1 tsp ground cinnamon

1 tsp ground ginger

175g unsalted butter,
  chilled

4 large eggs

TO SERVE

6 tbsp brandy

brandy or rum butter

pouring custard
  (see page 216)

with any liquid remaining from the soaked fruit and stir into the mixture with the lemon and orange zest.

4. Butter two 1.2 litre pudding basins (or decorative metal or porcelain jelly moulds). Divide the mixture equally between the two, smoothing the surface. Cover with pleated double greaseproof paper (this allows the pudding to expand whilst cooking), and top with a pleated sheet of foil. Secure with string and make a handle to help lift the puddings out of the pan(s).

5. Place the puddings in one or two large saucepans and pour in enough boiling water to come halfway up the sides of the basins. Cover and steam for 6 hours, checking the water level and topping up with boiling water as necessary. Do not let the pans boil dry. Cool completely, then wrap in fresh greaseproof paper and foil and store in a cool place until needed.

6. To serve, steam each pudding as before for 2 hours. Remove the papers and turn out onto a warmed serving dish. Heat the brandy in a small pan and pour over the pudding. Ignite with a match or taper and tip the plate from time to time to burn off all the alcohol. Serve with brandy or rum butter, or thin custard.

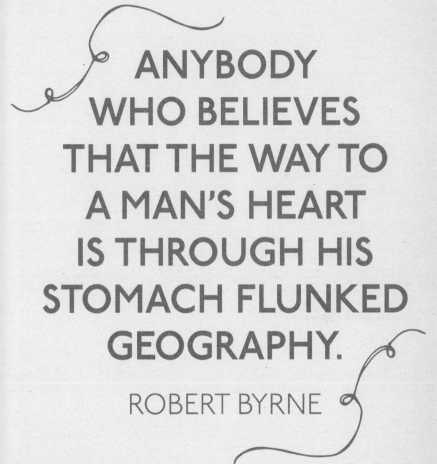

ANYBODY
WHO BELIEVES
THAT THE WAY TO
A MAN'S HEART
IS THROUGH HIS
STOMACH FLUNKED
GEOGRAPHY.

ROBERT BYRNE

SERENE SPONGES

Marbled Lemon Flower Cake

This is a very pretty cake. The inside has swirls of pink and yellow sponge and the lemon icing topping provides the perfect backdrop for a display of edible flowers.

SERVES 8

250g plain white flour

1½ tsp baking powder

½ tsp bicarbonate of soda

125g unsalted butter

200g caster sugar

3 eggs

200ml buttermilk

1 tsp vanilla extract

zest of 1 lemon

1 tbsp lemon juice

1 tsp rosewater

a few drops of pink food colouring

1. Preheat the oven to 180°C/Gas 4. Grease and flour a 25cm ring tin, with a depth of 5cm (see page 212). Sift the flour with the baking powder and bicarbonate of soda to thoroughly combine.

2. Beat the butter with an electric mixer until soft, then add the sugar. Continue to beat until very light and fluffy. Add the eggs one at a time, alternating with tablespoons of the flour mixture, then gently fold in the

FOR THE ICING

2 tbsp lemon juice

200g icing sugar, sifted

TO DECORATE

a selection of edible
   fresh, dried or
   crystallized flowers

rest of the flour. Stir in the buttermilk
and vanilla.

3. Take two-thirds of the batter and
mix in the zest and lemon juice. Add
the rosewater and pink food colouring
to the remaining third.

4. Pour the lemon batter into the
prepared cake tin and spread it out
evenly. Spoon the rose batter on top,
then smooth down and swirl through
with a skewer or knife to create a
marbled effect.

5. Bake for about 25 minutes, until
well risen and firm to the touch.
Remove from the oven, transfer to a
wire rack and leave to cool completely.

6. Meanwhile, make the icing. Whisk
the lemon juice into the icing sugar
and gradually add cold water, half
a teaspoon at a time, until it is the
desired consistency – you should be
able to drizzle it, rather than spread it.

7. When the cake has completely
cooled, drizzle over the icing and
decorate with the flowers.

A CAKE IS A VERY
GOOD TEST OF AN
OVEN: IF IT BROWNS
TOO MUCH ON ONE
SIDE AND NOT ON
THE OTHER, IT'S NOT
YOUR FAULT – YOU
NEED TO HAVE YOUR
OVEN CHECKED.

DELIA SMITH

ALMOND ANGEL CAKE

THIS CAKE HAS A LIGHT, BOUNCY CONSISTENCY, WHICH IS GIVEN TEXTURE BY THE ADDITION OF GROUND ALMONDS.

SERVES 8

60g plain white flour

15g cornflour

150g caster sugar

5 egg whites

½ tsp cream of tartar

½ tsp vanilla extract

¼ tsp almond extract

1 tsp lemon juice

75g ground almonds

TO SERVE

50g flaked almonds

250g summer fruits (a mixture of strawberries, raspberries and blueberries)

1. Preheat the oven to 180°C/Gas 4. Grease a shallow 25cm ring tin and then dust with flour.

2. Mix together plain flour and cornflour, then sift at least three times so they are very well combined and aerated. Add half the caster sugar and sift one last time.

3. Whisk the egg whites together until they form soft peaks. Add the cream of tartar, then gradually add the remaining sugar, whisking all the while until the mixture is stiff and glossy.

2 tbsp icing sugar

whipped cream or
crème fraîche

Add the vanilla extract, almond extract
and lemon juice.

4. Using a large metal spoon fold
in the dry ingredients, including the
ground almonds.

5. Spoon the mixture into the
prepared tin. Bake for 30–35 minutes
until golden brown with a springy
texture. Allow the cake to cool in the
tin for 10 minutes before turning out.

6. Toast the flaked almonds in a
dry frying pan until they turn a light
brown.

7. To assemble the cake pile the fruits
into the hollow centre of the angel
cake. Dust everything with icing sugar
and sprinkle the flaked almonds over
the top. Serve with whipped cream or
crème fraîche.

Maple Syrup and Pecan Cake

This is an excellent cake for enjoying in the autumn. Make sure your pear isn't too ripe, as it will make the cake soggy.

SERVES 8–10

350g plain white flour

2 tsp baking powder

½ tsp bicarbonate of soda

225g unsalted butter, softened

225g light muscovado sugar

4 eggs

125ml maple syrup

1 tbsp milk

50g pecans, finely chopped

1 firm pear, peeled, cored and finely chopped

1. Preheat the oven to 180°C/Gas 4. Grease and base line two deep 20cm round cake tins (see page 212). Sift together the plain flour, baking powder and bicarbonate of soda.

2. Beat together the butter and sugar until soft, fluffy and a very pale golden brown. Mix in the eggs, one at a time, alternating with spoonfuls of the flour mixture, then fold in the rest of the flour with a large metal spoon.

3. Drizzle in the maple syrup and the milk. You should have a good dropping

FOR THE TOPPING

100g mascarpone
  cheese

300ml double cream

2 tbsp maple syrup

½ tsp vanilla extract

TO DECORATE

50g pecan halves

consistency. Stir in the pecans and the chopped pear.

4. Scrape into the prepared tins and bake in the oven for about 30 minutes, until well risen, golden brown and firm to the touch. Allow to cool in their tins for 10 minutes before turning out onto a cooling rack.

5. To make the topping, beat the mascarpone cheese until soft and fluffy. In a separate bowl, whisk the double cream until thick and it has doubled in volume. Gently mix the mascarpone cheese and the double cream together, then add the maple syrup and vanilla extract.

6. To assemble, spread a third of the topping over one of the cakes and place the other cake on top. There should be enough icing left over to cover the top and sides of the entire cake. Decorate with the pecan halves.

Carrot Cake with Mascarpone Topping

IN THIS VERSION OF CARROT CAKE, BRAZIL NUTS
REPLACE THE MORE FAMILIAR WALNUTS AND MILD,
CREAMY MASCARPONE PROVIDES A DELICIOUS
SMOOTH FROSTING.

SERVE 8–10

225g unsalted butter, softened

225g caster sugar

175g self-raising white flour

1 tsp baking powder

½ tsp ground allspice

4 eggs

zest of 1 orange

1 tbsp orange juice

50g ground almonds

350g carrots, peeled and finely grated

1. Preheat the oven to 180°C/Gas 4. Grease and base line two 18cm round sandwich tins (see page 212). Dust the sides of the tins with flour and shake out the excess.

2. Cream the butter and sugar together in a bowl until light and fluffy. Sift the flour, baking powder and allspice into a bowl. Add the eggs, orange zest and juice, and the ground almonds; beat well. Stir in the grated carrots and chopped Brazil nuts.

125g Brazil nuts, coarsely chopped and toasted

FOR THE TOPPING

250g mascarpone or low-fat cream cheese

1 tsp finely grated orange zest (optional)

2 tbsp orange juice

2 tbsp icing sugar

3. Divide the mixture evenly between the two tins and level the surfaces. Bake for 35–40 minutes until risen and firm to the touch. Transfer to a wire rack to cool.

4. For the topping, beat the cheese, orange zest if using, orange juice and icing sugar together in a bowl until smooth. Use half to sandwich the cakes together. Spread the remainder over the top of the cake, swirling it attractively.

Raspberry and Pistachio Sandwich Cake

This cake is light, moist and exceptionally spongy. Pistachio nuts flavour the cake, while fresh raspberries and cream provide an irresistible filling.

SERVES 8–10

65g shelled pistachio nuts

225g self-raising white flour

2 tsp baking powder

4 eggs

225g caster sugar

225g unsalted butter, softened

1 tsp vanilla extract

1. Preheat the oven to 160°C/Gas 3. Grease and base line two 20cm round sandwich tins (see page 212). Put the pistachio nuts in a bowl and cover with boiling water. Leave for 1 minute, then drain and remove the skins. Finely chop the nuts.

2. Sift the flour and baking powder into a bowl. Add the eggs, sugar, butter and vanilla extract and beat, using an electric whisk, until pale and creamy. Stir in the chopped nuts.

FOR THE FILLING

5 tbsp raspberry jam
150ml double cream
125g raspberries

TO DECORATE

225g raspberries
25g pistachio nuts
icing sugar, for dusting
(optional)

3. Divide the mixture evenly between the tins and level the surfaces. Bake for about 30 minutes until well risen and firm to the touch. Turn out and leave to cool on a wire rack.

4. Heat the jam in a small pan until just melted then leave to cool. Place one cake layer on a serving plate. Whip the cream until just peaking and spread over the cake. Scatter with the raspberries, then spoon over the melted jam. Top with the second cake layer.

5. To decorate, scatter the raspberries over the cake. Skin the pistachios (as in step 1) and sprinkle over the top. Dust with icing sugar if desired, and keep in a cool place until ready to serve.

NOTE

THE MIXTURE SHOULD BE VERY SOFT AND DROP EASILY FROM A SPOON BEFORE BAKING. IF IT SEEMS A LITTLE STIFF, STIR IN A DASH OF MILK OR WATER.

LOVELY LEMON CAKE

THIS ZESTY LEMON CAKE IS PERFECT WITH A CUP
OF TEA FOR AN AFTERNOON TREAT. THE ADDITION
OF A LAYER OF LEMON CURD TAKES IT BEYOND A
NORMAL LEMON DRIZZLE CAKE.

SERVES 8–10

225g self-raising
 white flour

4 eggs

225g caster sugar

225g baking spread

zest and juice of
 1 lemon

150g lemon curd

FOR THE TOPPING

zest and juice of
 1 lemon

50g granulated sugar

1. Preheat the oven to 180°C/Gas 4.
Grease and base line two 20cm round
sandwich tins (see page 212).

2. Sift the flour into a large bowl.
Add the eggs, caster sugar and baking
spread and beat, using an electric
whisk, until pale and creamy.

3. Add the lemon zest and juice to the
cake mixture, and mix well.

4. Divide the mixture equally between
the tins and level the surfaces. Bake for
about 25 minutes, until a knife inserted

into the middle comes out clean and the cakes are golden and risen. Turn out and leave to cool on a wire rack.

5. Place one cake layer on a serving plate. Spread the lemon curd on top and top with the second cake. Prick the top cake layer all over with a skewer or cocktail stick.

6. To make the topping, mix the lemon zest with 25g of the sugar. Sprinkle the mixture on top of the cake.

7. In a small saucepan, gently heat the lemon juice with the remaining sugar. Cook over a low heat for a few minutes, stirring frequently, until you have a syrup. Pour on top of the sandwich cake, and serve.

RED VELVET CAKE

THIS CAKE IS A BIT OF A SHOWSTOPPER. THE
FOUR LAYERS OF DEEP RED SPONGE CAKE AND
CONTRASTING SNOW-WHITE CREAM CHEESE ICING
LOOK VERY DRAMATIC.

SERVES 12–14

375g plain white flour

50g cocoa powder

3 tsp baking powder

½ tsp bicarbonate
of soda

150g unsalted butter

300g caster sugar

50ml red food
colouring

2 tsp vanilla extract

3 eggs

275ml buttermilk

1 tsp cider vinegar

1. Preheat the oven to 180°C/Gas 4.
Grease and base line four 20cm
round sandwich tins (see page 212).
Sift together the flour, cocoa powder,
baking powder and bicarbonate of soda
a couple of times to make sure they
are very well combined and aerated.

2. Beat together the butter and sugar
until soft and fluffy, then add the food
colouring and the vanilla extract. Beat
again thoroughly.

3. Add the eggs one at a time,
alternating with the flour and cocoa

FOR THE CREAM CHEESE ICING

200g full-fat
  cream cheese

250g unsalted butter,
  softened

600g icing sugar, sifted

2 tsp vanilla extract

TO DECORATE

red sprinkles

powder mixture. Fold in the rest of the flour mixture, then finally mix in the buttermilk and the vinegar.

4. Divide the mixture between the prepared cake tins and level the surfaces. Bake for about 30 minutes until well risen and firm to the touch. A skewer inserted into the middle should come out clean.

5. For the cream cheese icing, beat together the cream cheese and butter until very soft and light, then gradually add in the icing sugar. This may feel quite stiff to start with, but keep beating and it will eventually soften and become extremely light and fluffy. Add the vanilla extract and beat for at least 5 minutes – this will ensure the icing is of sufficient volume to fill and cover the cake.

6. To assemble the cake, sandwich together all the layers with some of the icing, then cover the entire top and sides. Decorate lavishly with red sprinkles.

A GREAT EMPIRE, LIKE A GREAT CAKE, IS MOST EASILY DIMINISHED AT THE EDGES.

BENJAMIN FRANKLIN

TO ASCERTAIN WHEN THEY ARE DONE, PLUNGE A CLEAN KNIFE INTO THE MIDDLE, AND IF ON WITHDRAWAL IT COMES OUT CLEAN, THE CAKES ARE DONE.

MRS BEETON

Buttermilk
Pound Cake

THE BEAUTY OF A POUND CAKE IS ITS SIMPLICITY, AS IT IS TRADITIONALLY MADE WITH EQUAL QUANTITIES OF ALL THE MAIN INGREDIENTS. THIS VERSION HAS LESS BUTTER TO ALLOW FOR THE BUTTERMILK.

SERVES 8–10

225g self-raising white flour
150g unsalted butter
225g caster sugar, plus 2 tbsp
3 eggs
100ml buttermilk
1 tsp vanilla extract
zest of 1 lemon

1. Preheat the oven to 180°C/Gas 4. Grease and base line a deep 20cm round cake tin or a 1.5 litre loaf tin (see page 212). Sift the flour a couple of times to fully aerate it.

2. Beat the butter with an electric whisk until soft, then add the 225g of sugar. Continue to beat together until very light and fluffy. Mix in the eggs one at a time, alternating with tablespoons of the flour. Fold in the rest of the flour with a large metal spoon. Stir in the buttermilk, vanilla extract and lemon zest.

3. Scrape the batter into your prepared tin and sprinkle over the 2 tablespoons of sugar. Bake for about 50 minutes until golden brown and a skewer inserted into the middle comes out clean. Allow to cool in the tin for 10 minutes before turning out onto a wire rack.

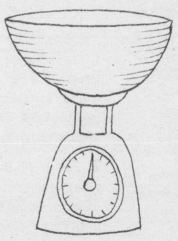

Vanilla Gugelhupf with Spiced Butter

RICH AND SWEET, WITH A LOVELY MOIST TEXTURE, THIS DELICIOUS BUTTERY CAKE IS SIMILAR TO A BRIOCHE. IT HAS A SUBTLE FLAVOURING OF VANILLA SUGAR, GLACÉ CHERRIES AND CITRUS PEEL.

SERVES 10

125g unsalted butter

250g plain white flour

a pinch of salt

2 tsp fast-action dried yeast

40g caster sugar

15g vanilla sugar (see page 216)

1 tsp vanilla extract

zest of 1 lemon

50g chopped mixed peel

25g glacé cherries, finely chopped

1. Melt the butter and leave to cool slightly. Sift the flour and salt into a bowl. Add the yeast, sugars, vanilla extract, lemon zest, chopped peel and cherries.

2. Beat the melted butter with the milk and eggs. Add to the bowl and beat well for 2 minutes. Cover the bowl with cling film and leave in a warm place until the mixture has doubled in size.

3 tbsp milk

3 eggs

FOR THE SPICE BUTTER

75g unsalted butter, softened

I tbsp icing sugar

¼ tsp ground nutmeg

½ tsp ground mixed spice

¼ tsp ground ginger

TO FINISH

icing sugar, for dusting

3. Meanwhile make the spice butter. Beat the ingredients together in a bowl until thoroughly combined. Transfer into a small serving dish and keep in a cool place.

4. Brush a 1.7 litre ring tin with a little melted butter. Dust with flour and shake out the excess.

5. Lightly beat the risen dough to reduce the volume, then turn into the prepared tin. Cover with oiled cling film and leave to rise until the dough almost reaches the top of the tin.

6. Preheat the oven to 200°C/Gas 6. Bake for 25–30 minutes until deep golden. Leave in the tin for 5 minutes, then loosen the edges with a knife. Invert the tin onto a wire rack and tap the cake out. Cool slightly before serving, dusted with icing sugar and accompanied by the spiced butter.

NOTE

ALTHOUGH THIS CAKE IS VERY EASY TO MAKE, DO ALLOW PLENTY OF TIME FOR THE DOUGH TO RISE. THIS MIGHT TAKE 2 HOURS FOR THE FIRST PROVING AND A FURTHER HOUR IN THE TIN.

COFFEE MARSALA CAKE WITH MARSALA CREAM

THIS IS A VERY GROWN-UP CAKE, REMINISCENT OF A BOOZY TIRAMISU. THE ADDITION OF COFFEE STOPS IT BEING OVERLY SWEET.

SERVES 8–10

225g self-raising white flour

1 tbsp instant espresso powder

225g unsalted butter

225g soft light brown sugar

4 eggs

1 tbsp Marsala wine

1 tsp vanilla extract

3 tbsp milk

1. Preheat the oven to 180°C/Gas 4. Grease and base line two deep 20cm round cake tins (see page 212). Sift the flour and espresso powder together.

2. Beat the butter with an electric whisk until soft, then add the sugar. Continue to beat together until light and fluffy. Mix in the eggs one at a time, alternating with tablespoons of the flour mixture. Gently fold in the remaining flour, then stir in all the liquids. You should have a soft, dropping consistency.

SERENE SPONGES

**FOR THE
MARSALA CREAM**

½ tsp instant
  espresso powder
300ml double cream
2 tbsp Marsala wine
1 tbsp icing sugar

3. Divide the batter between the prepared cake tins and level the surfaces. Bake for about 25 minutes, until well risen and firm to the touch. Leave the cakes to cool in their tins for 10 minutes, then turn out onto a wire rack.

4. To make the Marsala cream, dissolve the espresso powder in 1 tablespoon of boiling water. Whip the cream until thick and fairly stiff, then fold in the espresso, Marsala wine and the icing sugar. Mix together thoroughly, but lightly.

5. To assemble, place one of the cakes on a serving plate and spread with a third of the cream. Top with the remaining cake layer. Cover the top and side with the rest of the cream.

NOTE

DON'T BE TEMPTED TO SUBSTITUTE THE ESPRESSO POWDER WITH REGULAR INSTANT COFFEE POWDER.

TRANQUIL
TARTS

TREACLE TART

THIS ROBUST PUDDING ILLUSTRATES HOW THE
SIMPLEST INGREDIENTS CAN BE TRANSFORMED
INTO A MOST HEAVENLY DESSERT.

SERVES 8–10

225g plain white flour
150g unsalted butter
1 egg yolk
15g caster sugar

FOR THE FILLING

700g golden syrup
175g white
  breadcrumbs
zest of 3 lemons
2 eggs

TO SERVE

ice cream or
  crème fraîche

1. To make the pastry, sift the flour and put it in a food processor. Add the butter, cut into small pieces, and work until the mixture resembles breadcrumbs. Add the egg yolk, sugar and about 2 tablespoons of cold water. Process briefly to a firm dough. Turn out onto a lightly floured surface and knead lightly, then wrap in cling film and chill in the fridge for 30 minutes.

2. Preheat the oven to 180°C/Gas 4. Roll out the pastry on a lightly floured surface and use it to line a 25cm square fluted flan tin, with sides approximately 4cm deep (see page 215). Trim off the excess pastry and flute the edges. Prick the base with a fork.

3. For the filling, lightly heat the golden syrup in a saucepan until it has thinned in consistency. Remove from the heat and mix with the breadcrumbs and lemon zest. Lightly beat the eggs and stir into the syrup mixture. Pour the filling into the pastry case and smooth over.

4. Bake for 45–50 minutes until the filling is lightly set and turning golden. Allow to cool slightly. Serve warm, with ice cream or crème fraîche.

Tiramisu Torte

AN OUTRAGEOUSLY RICH DESSERT WITH AN IRRESISTIBLY GOOEY TEXTURE. A CREAMY RUM AND VANILLA MIXTURE IS MARBLED INTO DARK CHOCOLATE, COFFEE AND LIQUEUR, POURED INTO AN AMARETTI BISCUIT SHELL AND BAKED.

SERVES 8–10

275g amaretti biscuits or macaroons

125g unsalted butter

FOR THE FILLING

700g mascarpone or cream cheese (at room temperature)

150g caster sugar

3 eggs, separated

30g plain white flour

3 tbsp dark rum

½ tsp vanilla extract

1. Place the biscuits in a blender or food processor and process until finely ground. Melt 75g of the butter and stir in the crumbs until well coated. Spoon into a 23cm spring-release round cake tin. Press evenly over the base and 4cm up the sides with the back of a spoon to form a neat shell. Chill for at least 30 minutes until firm.

2. Preheat the oven to 200°C/Gas 6. Using a wooden spoon beat the mascarpone until smooth. Add the

175g dark chocolate (at least 70% cocoa solids)

1 tbsp instant espresso powder

3 tbsp Tia Maria or other coffee liqueur

TO FINISH

icing sugar, for dusting (optional)

TO SERVE

crème fraîche

sugar and beat again until quite smooth, then beat in the egg yolks. Divide the mixture in half and stir the flour, rum and vanilla into one half.

3. Break up the chocolate and melt it in a heatproof bowl set over a pan of simmering water (see page 218), cool slightly, then stir in the coffee powder and coffee liqueur. Stir into the remaining half of the soft cheese mixture. Whisk the egg whites until just holding soft peaks and fold half into each flavoured cheese mixture.

4. Quickly spoon alternate mounds of the two cheese mixtures into the firm biscuit case until full. Using a knife, swirl the mixtures together to produce a marbled effect.

5. Bake for 45 minutes, covering the top with foil if it appears to be over-browning. At this stage the torte will be soft in the middle. Leave in the switched-off oven with the door slightly ajar, to cool completely; it will continue to firm up during this time. Chill for several hours before serving, to allow the flavours to develop.

6. If desired, dust the top of the torte with icing sugar. Serve cut into wedges, with crème fraîche.

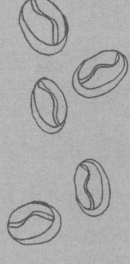

PART OF THE SECRET OF SUCCESS IN LIFE IS TO EAT WHAT YOU LIKE AND LET THE FOOD FIGHT IT OUT INSIDE.

MARK TWAIN

TARTE TATIN

THIS CLASSIC FRENCH DESSERT IS COOKED UPSIDE
DOWN. AFTER BAKING, THE TART IS TURNED OVER
SO THE FRUIT LAYER IS ON TOP AND THE BUTTERY,
CARAMEL JUICES OOZE INTO THE PASTRY.

SERVES 6

225g ready-made puff
pastry (or 1/3 of the
recipe on page 214)

FOR THE FILLING

75g caster sugar

4–5 eating apples

50g unsalted butter,
in pieces

TO SERVE

vanilla ice cream

1. First make the filling. Put the sugar in a saucepan with 3 tablespoons of water. Dissolve over a low heat, stirring occasionally, then increase the heat and without stirring, cook the syrup to a rich caramel. Carefully pour into a shallow heavy-based 20cm cake tin or an ovenproof frying pan and swirl around to coat the base of the tin evenly with caramel.

2. Preheat the oven to 220°C/Gas 7. Cut the apples in half, peel them and then scoop out the cores with a teaspoon.

3. Dot the caramel with half of the butter. Arrange the apple halves curved side down on top, packing them as tightly as possible. Fill any gaps with smaller wedges of apple. Dot the remaining butter on top. Place the tin or frying pan over a medium heat and cook for about 5 minutes to par-cook and lightly brown the apples. Watch carefully to make sure the apples do not burn.

4. Roll out the puff pastry on a lightly floured surface to form a round, slightly larger than the diameter of the tin or pan. Prick all over with a fork. Carefully lift the pastry round and place on top of the apples. Pat down gently, tucking the edges of the pastry down inside the sides of the tin. Bake for 20–25 minutes until the pastry is well risen, crisp and golden brown.

5. Allow to cool for 10 minutes. To remove the tart from the tin, cover it with a large inverted serving plate, carefully tip out any cooking juices into a bowl, then quickly turn the tin and plate over so that the plate is the right way up. Give the base of the tin a few sharp taps, then carefully lift it off the tart. Drizzle over the buttery juices and serve at once, cut into wedges, with a dollop or two of vanilla ice cream.

CUSTARD: A DETESTABLE SUBSTANCE PRODUCED BY A MALEVOLENT CONSPIRACY OF THE HEN, THE COW, AND THE COOK.

AMBROSE BIERCE

Raspberry and Vanilla Custard Tart

IN THIS SUMMER TART, SWEET RASPBERRIES SIT ATOP A CREAMY VANILLA CUSTARD, WITH A LIBERAL DUSTING OF VANILLA SUGAR.

SERVES 6

175g plain white flour
125g unsalted butter
25g vanilla sugar
  (see page 216)
1 tsp finely grated
  orange zest
1 egg yolk

FOR THE VANILLA CUSTARD

2 eggs
2 egg yolks
40g caster sugar
½ vanilla pod
450ml single cream

1. To make the pastry, sift the flour into a bowl. Rub in the butter, cut into small pieces, using your fingertips. Add the vanilla sugar and orange zest, then, using a round-bladed knife, mix in the egg yolk, together with 2–3 teaspoons of cold water to form a stiff dough.

2. Knead the pastry dough briefly until smooth. Wrap in cling film and chill in the fridge for 20 minutes.

3. Preheat the oven to 200°C/Gas 6. Butter a 20cm round, 4cm deep, loose-based fluted flan tin.

TO FINISH

175g raspberries

vanilla sugar,
  for dusting

4. Roll out the dough on a lightly floured surface and use it to line the prepared flan tin (see page 215). Chill again for 20 minutes. Line the pastry case with greaseproof paper or foil and baking beans and blind bake (see page 215) for 15 minutes. Remove the baking beans and paper or foil and return to the oven for 5–10 minutes to cook the base.

5. To make the custard filling beat the whole eggs, egg yolks and sugar in a bowl. Split the vanilla pod, scrape out the seeds and place both in a small pan with the cream. Cook over a very low heat until the cream is well flavoured and almost boiling. Pour onto the egg mixture, whisking constantly, then strain into the pastry case.

6. Lower the oven temperature to 150°C/Gas 2. Place the tart in the oven and bake for 45 minutes or until the centre is lightly set. Remove from the oven and leave until cold.

7. Carefully remove the flan from the tin. To finish, arrange the raspberries on top of the vanilla custard and dust liberally with vanilla sugar.

NOTE

TAKE CARE TO AVOID OVERCOOKING THE CUSTARD FILLING – IT SHOULD STILL WOBBLE SLIGHTLY IN THE CENTRE WHEN IT IS DONE.

Walnut Tart with Caramel Ice Cream

WALNUTS AND CARAMEL ARE A MARRIAGE MADE IN HEAVEN! WALNUTS ARE ENCASED IN AN IRRESISTIBLE GOOEY FUDGE MIXTURE IN THIS RIDICULOUSLY DELICIOUS TART.

SERVES 8–10

225g plain white flour

2 tbsp icing sugar

125g unsalted butter

2 egg yolks

FOR THE FILLING

125g unsalted
  butter, softened

125g light
  muscovado sugar

3 eggs

finely grated zest
  and juice of
  1 small orange

1. First make the ice cream. Put the sugar in a saucepan with 150ml water. Dissolve over a low heat until clear. Increase the heat and boil rapidly until the sugar begins to caramelize.

2. Remove from the heat and leave the caramel to stand for 2–3 minutes; it will turn a deep amber brown colour. Pour on the milk and cream, stirring, then whisk in the egg yolks. Return to a gentle heat and stir, without letting the custard boil, for about 15 minutes until

175g golden syrup
225g walnut pieces
a pinch of salt

**FOR THE CARAMEL
ICE CREAM**
225g granulated sugar
300ml milk
300ml double cream
8 egg yolks

slightly thickened. Allow to cool, then chill in the fridge.

3. Freeze the ice cream, using an ice cream machine if you have one. Alternatively, pour the mixture into a freezer-proof container and freeze until firm.

4. To make the pastry, sift the flour and icing sugar together into a bowl and rub in the butter. Stir in the egg yolks and enough iced water to bind to a firm dough. Knead lightly until smooth. Wrap in cling film and chill for 30 minutes.

5. Preheat the oven to 200°C/Gas 6. Roll out the pastry thinly and use it to line a 23cm round fluted flan tin (see page 215). Chill for 20 minutes. Line with greaseproof paper and baking beans and bake blind (see page 215) for 15–20 minutes, removing the paper and beans for the last 5 minutes. Lower the oven temperature to 180°C/Gas 4.

6. To make the filling, cream the butter and sugar together until light and fluffy. Gradually beat in the eggs, one at a time, then stir in the orange zest and juice. Heat the syrup until runny, but not very hot, then stir into the filling with the walnuts and salt. Pour into the flan case and bake for 40–45 minutes until lightly browned and risen. (The tart will sink a little on cooling.) Serve warm or cold, in slices with a scoop of the caramel ice cream.

LIFE IS UNCERTAIN. EAT DESSERT FIRST.

ERNESTINE ULMER

Ratafia Bakewell Tart

THIS RECIPE REVIVES ONE OF OUR MOST FAMOUS
PUDDINGS TO ITS ORIGINAL GLORY. HERE, A DEEP
ALMOND SPONGE AND THICK APRICOT CONSERVE
ARE ENCLOSED IN A DEEP-SIDED PASTRY CASE.

SERVES 8

225g plain white flour

50g lightly salted
butter

50g white
vegetable fat

FOR THE FILLING

4 tbsp apricot
conserve or jam

50g ratafia biscuits

75g unsalted butter

3 eggs

125g caster sugar

1 tsp almond essence

125g ground almonds

1. To make the pastry, sift the flour
into a bowl. Add the fats, cut into small
pieces, and rub in using your fingertips.
Stir in enough cold water to make a
firm dough. Knead lightly, then wrap in
cling film and chill for 30 minutes.

2. Preheat the oven to 200°C/Gas 6.
Preheat a baking tray. Roll out the
pastry on a lightly floured surface and
use it to line a 23cm spring-release
round cake tin (see page 212). Spread
the apricot conserve over the base.
Halve the ratafia biscuits.

caramel oranges
(see page 202),
optional

I tbsp icing sugar,
for dusting

cream or crème
fraîche

3. Melt the butter and set aside. Put the eggs and sugar in a large bowl and whisk until the mixture is thick enough to leave a trail on the surface when the whisk is lifted. Pour in the melted butter around the edge of the bowl. Add the almond essence and scatter over the ground almonds and ratafia biscuits. Fold in carefully, using a large metal spoon, until just combined.

4. Turn the mixture into the pastry-lined tin. Place on the preheated baking tray and bake for 10 minutes. Lower the oven temperature to 180°C/Gas 4 and bake for a further 40 minutes or until the filling is firm and set.

5. If serving with caramel oranges, arrange some on top of the tart, spooning a little of the syrup over them. Allow the tart to cool slightly, then remove from the tin and place on a serving place. Dust with icing sugar and serve with cream or crème fraîche and the rest of the oranges.

NOTE

DON'T WORRY IF THE TART SINKS SLIGHTLY IN THE CENTRE. THIS WILL ACCENTUATE ITS LOVELY CRACKED CRUST.

3 oranges
175g caster sugar

CARAMEL ORANGES

Pare strips of zest from 1 orange. Peel
3 oranges, discarding all the white pith,
then slice thinly. Dissolve 175g sugar in
600ml water in a heavy-based pan over
a low heat. Increase the heat and boil
steadily for 5 minutes. Add the orange
zest and slices. Bring to the boil, then
simmer gently for 15 minutes. Remove
the zest and fruit with a slotted spoon
and cook the syrup for a further 20
minutes until pale golden. Return the
fruit to the syrup. Allow to cool a little
before serving.

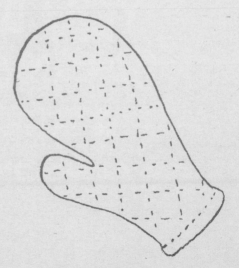

TRANQUIL TARTS

MARGE, IT'S 3 A.M.! SHOULDN'T YOU BE BAKING?

HOMER SIMPSON

Walnut and Orange Torte

THE TECHNIQUE OF FOLDING WHISKED EGG
WHITES INTO A CREAMED MIXTURE GIVES A
SOUFFLÉ-LIKE QUALITY TO THIS AIRY SPONGE.

SERVES 8–10

165g walnuts

150g unsalted butter, softened

150g caster sugar

5 eggs, separated

zest of 1 orange

150g ricotta cheese

40g plain white flour

1. Preheat the oven to 190°C/Gas 5. Grease and base line a 23cm spring-release round cake tin (see page 212). Lightly toast the walnuts, allow to cool, then chop roughly. Set aside 40g for the decoration.

2. Cream the butter and 125g of the sugar together in a bowl until light and fluffy. Add the egg yolks, orange zest, ricotta cheese, flour and roughly chopped walnuts. Mix gently until evenly combined.

TO FINISH

6 tbsp apricot jam

2 tsp orange juice

25g dark chocolate (at least 70% cocoa solids), in one piece (at room temperature)

3. Put the egg whites into another large bowl and whisk until stiff but not dry. Gradually whisk in the remaining sugar. Using a large metal spoon, fold a quarter into the cheese mixture to loosen it slightly, then carefully fold in the rest.

4. Turn the mixture into the prepared tin and gently level the surface. Bake for about 30 minutes until risen and just firm. Remove from the oven and leave to cool in the tin.

5. Heat the apricot jam in a pan until melted, then press through a sieve into a bowl and stir in the orange juice to make a glaze.

6. Brush half the apricot glaze around the side of the cake. Using a palette knife, coat the side of the cake with the reserved walnuts.

7. Brush the remaining apricot glaze over the top of the cake. Using a swivel vegetable peeler, shave simple curls from the chocolate and scatter over the top of the cake to serve (or, for long thin curls, see page 219).

VARIATION

OMIT THE CHOCOLATE CURLS. COVER THE TOP OF THE CAKE WITH HALVED AND STONED GREENGAGES OR SMALL PLUMS. GLAZE THE FRUIT WITH 4 TABLESPOONS OF WARMED AND SIEVED GREENGAGE OR PLUM JAM.

Rum, Raisin and White Chocolate Tart

THIS DELICIOUS TART HAS A LAYER OF RUM-
SOAKED RAISINS HIDDEN BENEATH A SPONGY
ALMOND TOPPING, WHICH IS HEAVILY SPECKLED
WITH CHUNKY PIECES OF WHITE CHOCOLATE.

SERVES 8

175g raisins

90ml rum

175g plain white flour

a pinch of salt

75g unsalted butter,
  in pieces

75g caster sugar

3 egg yolks

FOR THE FILLING

25g unblanched
  almonds

350g white chocolate

1. Put the raisins in a bowl, pour on the rum and leave to soak until most of the rum has been absorbed.

2. To make the pastry, sift the flour and salt into a large bowl. Rub in the butter until the mixture resembles breadcrumbs. Stir in the sugar and egg yolks, mixing to a smooth dough; add 1 teaspoon of cold water if necessary to bind the dough together. Knead lightly, wrap in cling film and chill for 30 minutes.

50g unsalted butter

125g light muscovado sugar

2 eggs

125g self-raising white flour

TO FINISH

1 tbsp icing sugar, for dusting

NOTE

IF YOU HAVE TIME, STEEP THE RAISINS IN THE RUM OVERNIGHT TO ALLOW THEM TO PLUMP UP THOROUGHLY.

3. Preheat the oven to 190°C/Gas 5. Roll out the pastry on a lightly floured surface and use it to line a 23cm loose-bottomed round flan tin (see page 215). Line the pastry case with greaseproof paper and fill with baking beans. Bake blind (see page 215) for 15 minutes, then remove the paper and beans and bake for a further 5 minutes. Leave to cool. Lower the oven temperature to 180°C/Gas 4.

4. Spoon the raisins and any rum into the pastry case. For the filling, roughly chop the almonds. Chop 300g of the white chocolate into small pieces.

5. Break up the remaining chocolate and put in a heatproof bowl set over a pan of simmering water (see page 218). Add the butter and leave until melted.

6. Beat the sugar and eggs together in a bowl. Stir in the flour, melted chocolate and three-quarters of the chopped chocolate. Turn into the flan case and sprinkle with the remaining chocolate and the almonds. Bake for 40 minutes until just firm, covering the tart with foil about halfway through cooking to prevent overbrowning. Serve warm, dusted with icing sugar.

Mincemeat Flan

The mincemeat needs to be prepared at least 2 weeks ahead to allow time to mature.

SERVES 10

50g blanched almonds

125g plain white flour

a pinch of salt

zest and juice of
 1 orange

50g caster sugar

50g unsalted butter,
 in pieces

1 egg yolk

3 medium bananas

2 tsp lemon juice

3 ripe star fruit

runny honey, for
 brushing

1. To make the mincemeat, core and grate the apple; roughly chop the cherries and nuts. Work the currants and sultanas in a food processor for 30 seconds, then stir into the apple mixture, together with the remaining ingredients. Mix well. Cover and leave to macerate for 2 days in a cool place. Pack into sterilized jars and seal.

2. For the pastry, toast the almonds until evenly golden. Allow to cool, then grind finely in a food processor.

3. Sift the flour and salt into a bowl and stir in the almonds, orange zest and sugar. Rub in the butter until the mixture resembles breadcrumbs. Beat

FOR THE MINCEMEAT

1 large cooking apple

50g glacé cherries

50g blanched almonds

225g currants

225g sultanas

125g chopped peel

225g soft dark
brown sugar

125g shredded suet

1 tsp ground cinnamon

½ tsp grated nutmeg

zest and juice of
1 orange

150ml brandy or rum

NOTE

THE BASIC
MINCEMEAT RECIPE
MAKES ABOUT 1.4KG,
WHICH IS MORE
THAN YOU WILL
NEED FOR THIS FLAN.
USE THE REST TO
MAKE INDIVIDUAL
MINCE PIES.

the egg yolk with 2 tablespoons of orange juice and stir into the mix until it begins to hold together; add more juice if necessary. Knead the dough lightly on a clean work surface until smooth. Wrap and chill for at least 1 hour. The pastry is quite crumbly.

4. Allow the pastry to come to room temperature. Peel the bananas, cut into cubes and toss in lemon juice. Mix with two-thirds of the mincemeat, then set aside.

5. Roll out the pastry and use it to line a 23cm round, 2.5cm deep fluted flan tin (see page 215). Chill for 15 minutes.

6. Preheat the oven to 190°C/Gas 5. Spoon the mincemeat and banana mixture evenly into the flan. Bake for 35–40 minutes until the pastry is golden brown.

7. Meanwhile, preheat the grill to high. Cut the star fruit into 0.5cm slices and place on a foil-lined grill pan. Brush with a little warmed honey and brown under the grill for 3–5 minutes; watch them closely! Allow to cool.

8. Decorate the flan with the star fruit and serve warm.

STEP-BY-STEP TECHNIQUES

Preparing Tins

To make most cakes it is necessary to line the tins with greaseproof paper or non-stick baking parchment. The latter is used for cakes that are more likely to stick, such as roulades and meringues.

Round

Place the tin on a piece of greaseproof paper or non-stick baking parchment and draw around it. Cut out, just inside the line. Cut strip(s) of paper, about 2cm wider than the depth of the tin. Fold up the bottom edge by Icm, then make cuts, 2.5cm apart, from edge to fold, all the way round. Grease the tin. Position the paper strip(s) around the side of the tin so that the snipped edge sits on the base. Lay the paper circle in the base, then grease all the paper.

Square or Rectangular

Cut a piece of greaseproof paper or non-stick baking parchment fractionally smaller than the base of the tin. For the sides, cut strips about 2cm wider than the depth of the tin. Fold up the bottom edge by Icm. Grease the tin. Make a cut from the edge of the paper to fold and press into one corner. Continue fitting the paper around the tin, cutting to fit at each corner. Lay the piece of paper in the base, then grease all the paper.

Loaf

Grease base and sides of the loaf tin. Cut a strip of greaseproof paper or non-stick baking parchment the length of the tin base and wide enough to cover the base and long sides. Press into position. Cut another strip, the width of the tin base and long enough to cover the base and ends of the tin. Press into position. Grease all the paper. Sometimes only the base and the long sides of a loaf tin need lining.

In this case, use a double thickness of paper so that the cake can easily be lifted from the tin.

SWISS ROLL

Grease the base and sides of the tin. Cut a rectangle of greaseproof paper or non-stick baking parchment, 7.5cm wider and longer than the size of the tin. Press the paper into the tin, cutting the paper at the corners and folding to fit neatly. Grease the paper.

SANDWICH

Place the sandwich tin on a piece of greaseproof paper or non-stick baking parchment and draw around it. Cut out, just inside the line. Grease the base and sides of the tin and fit the paper into the base. Grease the paper. Sprinkle a little flour into the tin. Tap and tilt the tin until the flour coats the base and sides. Tip out any excess flour.

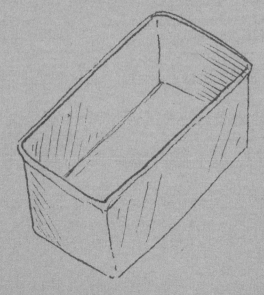

PUFF PASTRY

The richest of all the pastries, puff requires patience, practice and very light handling. Whenever possible it should be made the day before use. It is not practical to make in a quantity using less than 450g flour, but it can be frozen. Ready-made puff pastry is widely available, both fresh and frozen. This quantity is equivalent to two 375g packets of ready-made puff.

450G STRONG PLAIN WHITE FLOUR
A PINCH OF SALT
450G UNSALTED BUTTER, CHILLED
1 TBSP LEMON JUICE

1. Mix the flour and salt together in a bowl. Slice off 50g of the butter and cut into dice. Flatten the remaining butter with a rolling pin to form a slab 2cm thick.

2. Rub the diced butter into the flour. Using a round-bladed knife, stir in the lemon juice and about 300ml chilled water or sufficient to make a soft dough.

3. Quickly knead the dough until smooth and shape into a round. Cut through half the depth in the shape of a cross. Open out to form a star.

4. Roll out, keeping the centre four times as thick as the flaps. Place the slab of butter in the centre.

5. Fold the flaps envelope-style gently with a rolling pin. Roll out to a 40cm x 20cm rectangle.

6. Fold the bottom third up and the top third down, keeping the edges straight. Seal the edges. Wrap in cling film and leave to rest in the fridge for 30 minutes.

7. Place the pastry on a lightly floured surface with the folded edges to the sides, then repeat the rolling, folding and resting sequence five times.

Lining a Flan Case

Loose-based metal flan tins are ideal because they transfer heat rapidly and the pastry tends to cook better than in china dishes. The removable base makes it easier to transfer the baked flan to a serving plate. Alternatively, use a flat ring placed on a baking sheet, a sandwich tin or a fluted china flan dish.

1. Roll out the pastry on a lightly floured surface until it is about 5cm larger than the flan tin all the way round. Use the rolling pin to help you lift the pastry over the flan tin.

2. Lift the edges of the pastry so that it falls down into the tin, then gently press the pastry against the edges of the flan tin so that there are no gaps between the pastry and the tin.

3. Turn any surplus pastry outwards over the rim of the flan tin and trim the pastry edges with a sharp knife to neaten. Alternatively, you can roll the rolling pin over the top of the tin to cut off excess pastry.

Baking Blind

If a recipe instructs you to bake blind, it means that you should bake the pastry case (or cases) without any filling. The pastry may be partially cooked before adding the filling, or it may be completely cooked if the filling doesn't require further cooking. Fully baked pastry cases will keep for several days in an airtight tin or they may be frozen.

1. Line the flan tin or dish with pastry (see above). If you have time, chill the pastry case in the fridge for 20–30 minutes to rest the pastry and help reduce shrinkage during cooking. Prick the pastry base with a fork, then line with a piece of greaseproof paper or foil larger than the pastry case.

2. Fill with ceramic baking beans or dried pulses. Tartlet cases don't need lining; it should be sufficient to prick them with a fork.

3. For partially baked cases, bake at 200°C/Gas 6 for 10–15 minutes until the case looks 'set'. Carefully remove the paper or foil and the beans and bake for a further 5 minutes until the base is firm to the touch and lightly coloured. Pastry cases that require complete baking should be returned to the oven for about 15 minutes until firm and golden brown.

MAKING CUSTARD

This is a recipe for making 'real' custard. It can also form the basis of several creamy desserts.

3 EGG YOLKS
2 TBSP CASTER SUGAR
½ TSP CORNFLOUR
300ML MILK
½ TSP VANILLA EXTRACT

> **NOTE**
> A TRADITIONAL EGG CUSTARD DOESN'T INCLUDE CORNFLOUR, BUT YOU WILL FIND THAT INCORPORATING A LITTLE GREATLY REDUCES THE RISK OF CURDLING.

1. Place the egg yolks, sugar and cornflour in a bowl with a little of the milk and whisk until smooth.

2. Bring the milk to the boil in a heavy-based saucepan. Pour the milk onto the egg yolk mixture, whisking well. Return to the saucepan and add the vanilla extract.

3. Cook over the lowest possible heat, stirring constantly, for about 10 minutes until the custard thickens slightly. It should be thick enough to thinly coat the back of the wooden spoon. Do not boil, otherwise the custard may curdle. Strain and serve.

VANILLA SUGAR

To make your own vanilla sugar, simply bury a vanilla pod in a jar of caster sugar and leave it for a couple of days before using the sugar. The sugar level can be topped up as you use it.

If you haven't any vanilla sugar to hand, replace with ordinary caster sugar and a generous splash of vanilla extract.

COVERING A CAKE WITH MARZIPAN

1. Trim the top of the cake so that it is level. Turn the cake over so that the flat bottom becomes the top.

2. On a surface dusted with icing sugar, roll out half the marzipan to fit the top of the cake. Brush the cake top with apricot glaze (melted jam).

3. Lift the marzipan onto the top of the cake and smooth over, neatening the edges. Place on a cake board, which should be at least 5cm larger than the cake.

4. Cut a piece of string the same height as the cake with its marzipan top, and another to fit around the cake. Roll out the remaining marzipan and, using the string as a guide, trim the paste to size. Brush the side(s) of the cake and the marzipan rim at the top with apricot glaze.

5. Roll up the marzipan strip loosely. Place one end against the side of the cake and unroll to cover all the way round the cake. Use a palette knife to smooth over, and blend the joins of the paste.

6. Flatten the top lightly with a rolling pin. Leave the cake in a cool, dry room to dry out thoroughly for about 2 days before applying the icing.

APPLYING SUGARPASTE

1. Dust your work surface and rolling pin with cornflour. Knead the icing until pliable. Roll out into a round or square 5–7.5cm larger than the cake all the way round.

2. With the help of a rolling pin, lift the icing over the top of the cake and allow it to drape over the edges. Dust your hands with cornflour and press the icing onto the top and sides of the cake, easing it down to the board.

3. Trim off excess icing at the base.

4. With your fingers dusted with a little cornflour, gently rub the surface in a circular movement to buff the icing and make it smooth.

MELTING CHOCOLATE

ON THE HOB

Break the chocolate into pieces and place in a heatproof bowl. Place over a pan of gently simmering water and leave until melted (make sure the base of the bowl doesn't touch the simmering water). Once melted, gently stir the chocolate until completely smooth. Remove the bowl from the pan, ensuring that water droplets on the bowl do not come into contact with the chocolate.

IN THE MICROWAVE

Break the chocolate into pieces and place it in a small heatproof bowl. The time will vary according to the initial temperature of the chocolate, the amount used, and the type of bowl. As a guide, microwave dark or milk chocolate on High, allowing about 2 minutes for 125g chocolate and 3 minutes for 175–225g. White chocolate is best melted on Medium, as it is more likely to overheat.

CHOCOLATE CURLS

Spread melted chocolate on a marble slab or clean work surface and leave to set until no longer sticky to the touch. Holding a large knife at a slight angle to the surface, push the blade across the chocolate to shave off long thin curls. Adjust the angle of the blade to obtain the best curls. If the chocolate breaks into brittle pieces, then it has become too cold and should be left to soften before trying again.

For simple chocolate curls, use a large chunky bar of chocolate at room temperature and shave off curls using a swivel vegetable peeler.

DIPPED FRUITS AND NUTS

Choose small, whole fruits that are ripe but not soft. Strawberries, cherries, grapes, kumquats and gooseberries are ideal. Brazil nuts and pecans work well too. Wash the fruit if necessary and dry thoroughly.

1. Melt a little chocolate in a small bowl (see facing page). Half-dip the fruit and/or nuts in the chocolate, letting the excess chocolate drip back into the bowl.

2. Place the dipped fruits on a sheet of greaseproof paper to set.

INDEX

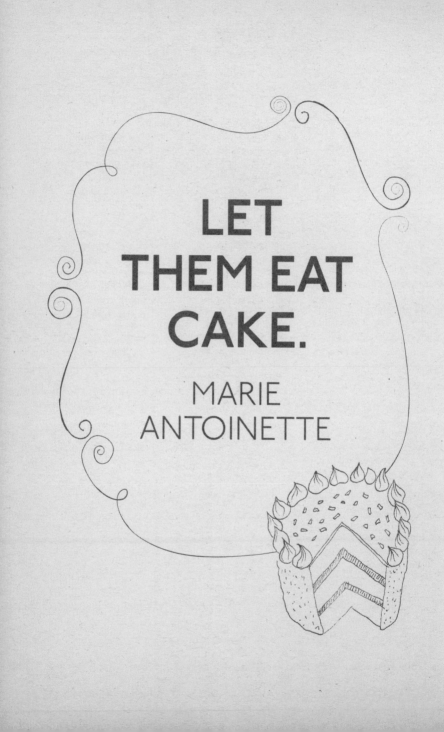

LET
THEM EAT
CAKE.

MARIE
ANTOINETTE

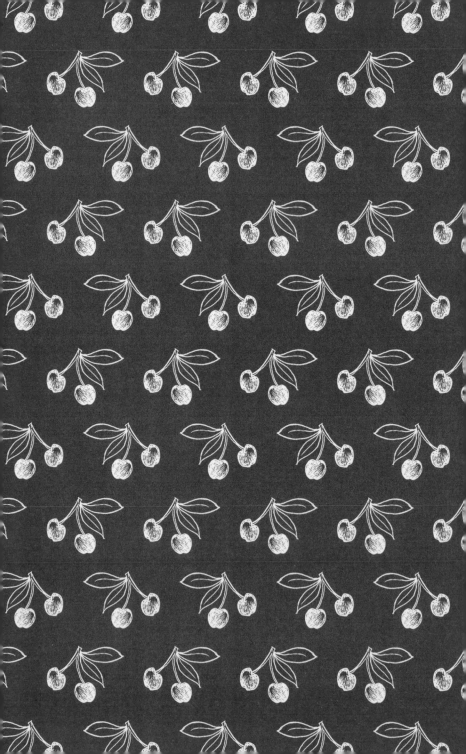